Martin Luther's Ninety-Five Theses and Selected Sermons

Martin Luther's Ninety-Five Theses and Selected Sermons

by Martin Luther

A & D Publishing
PO Box 3005
Radford VA 24143-3005
www.wilderpublications.com

ISBN 10: 1-60459-345-8
ISBN 13: 978-1-60459-345-7

First Edition

Table of Contents

Martin Luther's Ninety-Five Theses

October 31, 1517

Disputation of Doctor Martin Luther on the Power and Efficacy of Indulgences

Out of love for the truth and the desire to bring it to light, the following propositions will be discussed at Wittenberg, under the presidency of the Reverend Father Martin Luther, Master of Arts and of Sacred Theology, and Lecturer in Ordinary on the same at that place. Wherefore he requests that those who are unable to be present and debate orally with us, may do so by letter.

In the Name our Lord Jesus Christ. Amen.

1. Our Lord and Master Jesus Christ, when He said Poenitentiam agite, willed that the whole life of believers should be repentance.

2. This word cannot be understood to mean sacramental penance, i.e., confession and satisfaction, which is administered by the priests.

3. Yet it means not inward repentance only; nay, there is no inward repentance which does not outwardly work divers mortifications of the flesh.

4. The penalty [of sin], therefore, continues so long as hatred of self continues; for this is the true inward repentance, and continues until our entrance into the kingdom of heaven.

5. The pope does not intend to remit, and cannot remit any penalties other than those which he has imposed either by his own authority or by that of the Canons.

6. The pope cannot remit any guilt, except by declaring that it has been remitted by God and by assenting to God's remission; though, to be sure, he may grant remission in cases reserved to his judgment. If his right to grant remission in such cases were despised, the guilt would remain entirely unforgiven.

7. God remits guilt to no one whom He does not, at the same time, humble in all things and bring into subjection to His vicar, the priest. 8. The penitential

canons are imposed only on the living, and, according to them, nothing should be imposed on the dying.

9. Therefore the Holy Spirit in the pope is kind to us, because in his decrees he always makes exception of the article of death and of necessity.

10. Ignorant and wicked are the doings of those priests who, in the case of the dying, reserve canonical penances for purgatory.

11. This changing of the canonical penalty to the penalty of purgatory is quite evidently one of the tares that were sown while the bishops slept.

12. In former times the canonical penalties were imposed not after, but before absolution, as tests of true contrition.

13. The dying are freed by death from all penalties; they are already dead to canonical rules, and have a right to be released from them.

14. The imperfect health [of soul], that is to say, the imperfect love, of the dying brings with it, of necessity, great fear; and the smaller the love, the greater is the fear.

15. This fear and horror is sufficient of itself alone (to say nothing of other things) to constitute the penalty of purgatory, since it is very near to the horror of despair.

16. Hell, purgatory, and heaven seem to differ as do despair, almost-despair, and the assurance of safety.

17. With souls in purgatory it seems necessary that horror should grow less and love increase.

18. It seems unproved, either by reason or Scripture, that they are outside the state of merit, that is to say, of increasing love.

19. Again, it seems unproved that they, or at least that all of them, are certain or assured of their own blessedness, though we may be quite certain of it.

20. Therefore by "full remission of all penalties" the pope means not actually "of all," but only of those imposed by himself.

21. Therefore those preachers of indulgences are in error, who say that by the pope's indulgences a man is freed from every penalty, and saved;

22. Whereas he remits to souls in purgatory no penalty which, according to the canons, they would have had to pay in this life. 23. If it is at all possible to grant to any one the remission of all penalties whatsoever, it is certain that this remission can be granted only to the most perfect, that is, to the very fewest.

24. It must needs be, therefore, that the greater part of the people are deceived by that indiscriminate and highsounding promise of release from penalty.

25. The power which the pope has, in a general way, over purgatory, is just like the power which any bishop or curate has, in a special way, within his own diocese or parish.

26. The pope does well when he grants remission to souls [in purgatory], not by the power of the keys (which he does not possess), but by way of intercession.

27. They preach man who say that so soon as the penny jingles into the money-box, the soul flies out [of purgatory].

28. It is certain that when the penny jingles into the money-box, gain and avarice can be increased, but the result of the intercession of the Church is in the power of God alone.

29. Who knows whether all the souls in purgatory wish to be bought out of it, as in the legend of Sts. Severinus and Paschal.

30. No one is sure that his own contrition is sincere; much less that he has attained full remission.

31. Rare as is the man that is truly penitent, so rare is also the man who truly buys indulgences, i.e., such men are most rare.

32. They will be condemned eternally, together with their teachers, who believe themselves sure of their salvation because they have letters of pardon.

33. Men must be on their guard against those who say that the pope's pardons are that inestimable gift of God by which man is reconciled to Him;

34. For these "graces of pardon" concern only the penalties of sacramental satisfaction, and these are appointed by man.

35. They preach no Christian doctrine who teach that contrition is not necessary in those who intend to buy souls out of purgatory or to buy confessionalia.

36. Every truly repentant Christian has a right to full remission of penalty and guilt, even without letters of pardon.

37. Every true Christian, whether living or dead, has part in all the blessings of Christ and the Church; and this is granted him by God, even without letters of pardon.

38. Nevertheless, the remission and participation [in the blessings of the Church] which are granted by the pope are in no way to be despised, for they are, as I have said, the declaration of divine remission.

39. It is most difficult, even for the very keenest theologians, at one and the same time to commend to the people the abundance of pardons and [the need of] true contrition.

40. True contrition seeks and loves penalties, but liberal pardons only relax penalties and cause them to be hated, or at least, furnish an occasion [for hating them].

41. Apostolic pardons are to be preached with caution, lest the people may falsely think them preferable to other good works of love.

42. Christians are to be taught that the pope does not intend the buying of

pardons to be compared in any way to works of mercy.

43. Christians are to be taught that he who gives to the poor or lends to the needy does a better work than buying pardons;

44. Because love grows by works of love, and man becomes better; but by pardons man does not grow better, only more free from penalty.

45. Christians are to be taught that he who sees a man in need, and passes him by, and gives [his money] for pardons, purchases not the indulgences of the pope, but the indignation of God.

46. Christians are to be taught that unless they have more than they need, they are bound to keep back what is necessary for their own families, and by no means to squander it on pardons.

47. Christians are to be taught that the buying of pardons is a matter of free will, and not of commandment.

48. Christians are to be taught that the pope, in granting pardons, needs, and therefore desires, their devout prayer for him more than the money they bring.

49. Christians are to be taught that the pope's pardons are useful, if they do not put their trust in them; but altogether harmful, if through them they lose their fear of God.

50. Christians are to be taught that if the pope knew the exactions of the pardon-preachers, he would rather that St. Peter's church should go to ashes, than that it should be built up with the skin, flesh and bones of his sheep.

51. Christians are to be taught that it would be the pope's wish, as it is his duty, to give of his own money to very many of those from whom certain hawkers of pardons cajole money, even though the church of St. Peter might have to be sold.

52. The assurance of salvation by letters of pardon is vain, even though the commissary, nay, even though the pope himself, were to stake his soul upon it.

53. They are enemies of Christ and of the pope, who bid the Word of God be altogether silent in some Churches, in order that pardons may be preached in others.

54. Injury is done the Word of God when, in the same sermon, an equal or a longer time is spent on pardons than on this Word.

55. It must be the intention of the pope that if pardons, which are a very small thing, are celebrated with one bell, with single processions and ceremonies, then the Gospel, which is the very greatest thing, should be preached with a hundred bells, a hundred processions, a hundred ceremonies.

56. The "treasures of the Church," out of which the pope. grants indulgences, are not sufficiently named or known among the people of Christ.

57. That they are not temporal treasures is certainly evident, for many of the vendors do not pour out such treasures so easily, but only gather them.

58. Nor are they the merits of Christ and the Saints, for even without the pope, these always work grace for the inner man, and the cross, death, and hell for the outward man.

59. St. Lawrence said that the treasures of the Church were the Church's poor, but he spoke according to the usage of the word in his own time.

60. Without rashness we say that the keys of the Church, given by Christ's merit, are that treasure;

61. For it is clear that for the remission of penalties and of reserved cases, the power of the pope is of itself sufficient.

62. The true treasure of the Church is the Most Holy Gospel of the glory and the grace of God.

63. But this treasure is naturally most odious, for it makes the first to be last.

64. On the other hand, the treasure of indulgences is naturally most acceptable, for it makes the last to be first.

65. Therefore the treasures of the Gospel are nets with which they formerly were wont to fish for men of riches.

66. The treasures of the indulgences are nets with which they now fish for the riches of men.

67. The indulgences which the preachers cry as the "greatest graces" are known to be truly such, in so far as they promote gain.

68. Yet they are in truth the very smallest graces compared with the grace of God and the piety of the Cross.

69. Bishops and curates are bound to admit the commissaries of apostolic pardons, with all reverence.

70. But still more are they bound to strain all their eyes and attend with all their ears, lest these men preach their own dreams instead of the commission of the pope.

71. He who speaks against the truth of apostolic pardons, let him be anathema and accursed!

72. But he who guards against the lust and license of the pardon-preachers, let him be blessed!

73. The pope justly thunders against those who, by any art, contrive the injury of the traffic in pardons.

74. But much more does he intend to thunder against those who use the pretext of pardons to contrive the injury of holy love and truth.

75. To think the papal pardons so great that they could absolve a man even if he had committed an impossible sin and violated the Mother of God — this is madness.

76. We say, on the contrary, that the papal pardons are not able to remove the

very least of venial sins, so far as its guilt is concerned.

77. It is said that even St. Peter, if he were now Pope, could not bestow greater graces; this is blasphemy against St. Peter and against the pope.

78. We say, on the contrary, that even the present pope, and any pope at all, has greater graces at his disposal; to wit, the Gospel, powers, gifts of healing, etc., as it is written in I. Corinthians xii.

79. To say that the cross, emblazoned with the papal arms, which is set up [by the preachers of indulgences], is of equal worth with the Cross of Christ, is blasphemy.

80. The bishops, curates and theologians who allow such talk to be spread among the people, will have an account to render. 81. This unbridled preaching of pardons makes it no easy matter, even for learned men, to rescue the reverence due to the pope from slander, or even from the shrewd questionings of the laity.

82. To wit: — "Why does not the pope empty purgatory, for the sake of holy love and of the dire need of the souls that are there, if he redeems an infinite number of souls for the sake of miserable money with which to build a Church? The former reasons would be most just; the latter is most trivial."

83. Again: — "Why are mortuary and anniversary masses for the dead continued, and why does he not return or permit the withdrawal of the endowments founded on their behalf, since it is wrong to pray for the redeemed?"

84. Again: — "What is this new piety of God and the pope, that for money they allow a man who is impious and their enemy to buy out of purgatory the pious soul of a friend of God, and do not rather, because of that pious and beloved soul's own need, free it for pure love's sake?"

85. Again: — "Why are the penitential canons long since in actual fact and through disuse abrogated and dead, now satisfied by the granting of indulgences, as though they were still alive and in force?"

86. Again: — "Why does not the pope, whose wealth is to-day greater than the riches of the richest, build just this one church of St. Peter with his own money, rather than with the money of poor believers?"

87. Again: — "What is it that the pope remits, and what participation does he grant to those who, by perfect contrition, have a right to full remission and participation?"

88. Again: — "What greater blessing could come to the Church than if the pope were to do a hundred times a day what he now does once, and bestow on every believer these remissions and participations?"

89. "Since the pope, by his pardons, seeks the salvation of souls rather than money, why does he suspend the indulgences and pardons granted heretofore, since these have equal efficacy?"

90. To repress these arguments and scruples of the laity by force alone, and not to resolve them by giving reasons, is to expose the Church and the pope to the ridicule of their enemies, and to make Christians unhappy.

91. If, therefore, pardons were preached according to the spirit and mind of the pope, all these doubts would be readily resolved; nay, they would not exist.

92. Away, then, with all those prophets who say to the people of Christ, "Peace, peace," and there is no peace!

93. Blessed be all those prophets who say to the people of Christ, "Cross, cross," and there is no cross!

94. Christians are to be exhorted that they be diligent in following Christ, their Head, through penalties, deaths, and hell;

95. And thus be confident of entering into heaven rather through many tribulations, than through the assurance of peace.

Christ's Holy Sufferings

The True and the False Views of Christ's Sufferings

Section I. the False Views of Christ's Sufferings.

1. In the first place, some reflect upon the sufferings of Christ in a way that they become angry at the Jews, sing and lament about poor Judas, and are then satisfied; just like by habit they complain of other persons, and condemn and spend their time with their enemies. Such an exercise may truly be called a meditation not on the sufferings of Christ, but on the wickedness of Judas and the Jews.

2. In the second place, others have pointed out the different benefits and fruits springing from a consideration of Christ's Passion. Here the saying ascribed to Albertus is misleading, that to think once superficially on the sufferings of Christ is better than to fast a whole year or to pray the Psalter every day, etc. The people thus blindly follow him and act contrary to the true fruits of Christ's Passion; for they seek therein their own selfish interests. Therefore they decorate themselves with pictures and booklets, with letters and crucifixes, and some go so far as to imagine that they thus protect themselves against the perils of water, of fire, and of the sword, and all other dangers. In this way the suffering of Christ is to work in them an absence of suffering, which is contrary to its nature and character.

3. A third class so, sympathize with Christ as to weep and lament for him because he was so innocent, like the women who followed Christ from Jerusalem, whom he rebuked, in that they should better weep for themselves and for their children. Such are they who run far away in the midst of the Passion season, and are greatly benefited by the departure of Christ from Bethany and by the pains and sorrows of the Virgin Mary, but they never get farther. Hence they postpone the Passion many hours, and God only knows whether it is devised more for sleeping than for watching. And among these fanatics are those who taught what great blessings come from the holy mass, and in their simple way they think it is enough if they attend mass. To this we are led through the sayings of certain teachers, that the mass opere operati, non opere operantis, is acceptable of itself, even without our merit and worthiness, just as if that were enough. Nevertheless the mass was not instituted for the sake of its own worthiness but to prove us, especially for the purpose of

meditating upon the sufferings of Christ. For where this is not done, we make a temporal, unfruitful work out of the mass, however good it may be in itself. For what help is it to you, that God is God, if he is not God to you? What benefit is it that eating and drinking are in themselves healthful and good, if they are not healthful for you, and there is fear that we never grow better by reason of our many masses, if we fail to seek the true fruit in them?

Section II. The True View of Christ's Sufferings.

4. Fourthly, they meditate on the Passion of Christ aright, who so view Christ that they become terror-stricken in heart at the sight, and their conscience at once sinks in despair. This terror-stricken feeling should spring forth, so that you see the severe wrath and the unchangeable earnestness of God in regard to sin and sinners, in that he was unwilling that his only and dearly beloved Son should set sinners free unless he paid the costly ransom for them as is mentioned in Is 53:8: "For the transgression of my people was he stricken." What happens to the sinner, when the dear child is thus stricken? An earnestness must be present that is inexpressible and unbearable, which a person so immeasurably great goes to meet, and suffers and dies for it; and if you reflect upon it real deeply, that God's Son, the eternal wisdom of the Father, himself suffers, you will indeed be terror-stricken; and the more you reflect the deeper will be the impression.

5. Fifthly, that you deeply believe and never doubt the least, that you are the one who thus martyred Christ. For your sins most surely did it. Thus St. Peter struck and terrified the Jews as with a thunderbolt in Acts 2:36-37, when he spoke to them all in common: "Him have ye crucified," so that three thousand were terror-stricken the same day and tremblingly cried to the apostles: "O beloved brethren what shall we do?" Therefore, when you view the nails piercing through his hands, firmly believe it is your work. Do you behold his crown of thorns, believe the thorns are your wicked thoughts, etc.

6. Sixthly, now see, where one thorn pierces Christ, there more than a thousand thorns should pierce thee, yea, eternally should they thus and even more painfully pierce thee. Where one nail is driven through his hands and feet, thou shouldest eternally suffer such and even more painful nails; as will be also visited upon those who, let Christ's sufferings be lost and fruitless as far as they are concerned. For this earnest mirror, Christ, will neither lie nor mock; whatever he says must be fully realized.

7. Seventhly, St. Bernard was so terror-stricken by Christ's sufferings that he said: I imagined I was secure and I knew nothing of the eternal judgment passed upon me in heaven, until I saw that the eternal Son of God took mercy upon me, stepped forward and offered himself on my behalf in the same judgment. Ah, it does not become me still to play and remain secure when such earnestness, is behind those sufferings. Hence he commanded the women: "Weep not for me, but weep for yourselves, and for your children." Lk. 23:28;

and gives in the 31st verse the reason: "For if they do these things in the green tree, what shall be done in the dry?" As if to say: Learn from my martyrdom what you have merited and how you should be rewarded. For here it is true that a little dog was slain in order to terrorize a big one. Likewise the prophet also said: "All generations shall lament and bewail themselves more than him"; it is not said they shall lament him, but themselves rather than him. Likewise were also the apostles terror-stricken in Acts 2:27, as mentioned before, so that they said to the apostles: "O, brethren, what shall we do?" So the church also sings: I will diligently meditate thereon, and thus my soul in me will exhaust itself.

8. Eighthly, one must skilfully exercise himself in this point, for the benefit of Christ's sufferings depends almost entirely upon man coming to a true knowledge of himself, and becoming terror-stricken and slain before himself. And where man does not come to this point, the sufferings of Christ have become of no true benefit to him. For the characteristic, natural work of Christ's sufferings is that they make all men equal and alike, so that as Christ was horribly martyred as to body and soul in our sins, we must also like him be martyred in our consciences by our sins. This does not take place by means of many words, but by means of deep thoughts and a profound realization of our sins. Take an illustration: If an evil-doer were judged because he had slain the child of a prince or king, and you were in safety, and sang and played, as if you were entirely innocent, until one seized you in a horrible manner and convinced you that you had enabled the wicked person to do the act; behold, then you would be in the greatest straits, especially if your conscience also revolted against you. Thus much more anxious you should be, when you consider Christ's sufferings. For the evil doers, the Jews, although they have now judged and banished God, they have still been the servants of your sins, and you are truly the one who strangled and crucified the Son of God through your sins, as has been said.

9. Ninthly, whoever perceives himself to be so hard and sterile that he is not terror-stricken by Christ's sufferings and led to a knowledge of him, he should fear and tremble. For it cannot be otherwise; you must become like the picture and sufferings of Christ, be it realized in life or in hell; you must at the time of death, if not sooner, fall into terror, tremble, quake and experience all Christ suffered on the cross. It is truly terrible to attend to this on your deathbed; therefore you should pray God to soften your heart and permit you fruitfully to meditate upon Christ's Passion. For it is impossible for us profoundly to meditate upon the sufferings of Christ of ourselves, unless God sink them into our hearts. Further, neither this meditation nor any other doctrine is given to you to the
end that you should fall fresh upon it of yourself, to accomplish the same; but you are first to seek and long for the grace of God, that you may accomplish it through God's grace and not through your own power. For in this way it

happens that those referred to above never treat the sufferings of Christ aright; for they never call upon God to that end, but devise out of their own ability their own way, and treat those sufferings entirely in a human and an unfruitful manner.

10 Tenthly, whoever meditates thus upon God's sufferings for a day, an hour, yea, for a quarter of an hour, we wish to say freely and publicly, that it is better than if he fasts a whole year, prays the Psalter every day, yea, than if he hears a hundred masses. For such a meditation changes a man's character and almost as in baptism he is born again, anew. Then Christ's suffering accomplishes its true, natural and noble work, it slays the old Adam, banishes all lust, pleasure and security that one may obtain from God's creatures; just like Christ was forsaken by all, even by God.

11. Eleventhly, since then such a work is not in our hands, it happens that sometimes we pray and do not receive it at the time; in spite of this one should not despair nor cease to pray. At times it comes when we are not praying for it, as God knows and wills; for it will be free and unbound: then man is distressed in conscience and is wickedly displeased with his own life, and it may easily happen that he does not know that Christ's Passion is working this very thing in him, of which perhaps he was not aware, just like the others so exclusively meditated on Christ's Passion that in their knowledge of self they could not extricate themselves out of that state of meditation. Among the first the sufferings of Christ are quite and true, among the others a show and false, and according to its nature God often turns the leaf, so that those who do not meditate on the Passion, really do, meditate on it; and those who bear the mass, do not hear it; and those who hear it not, do hear it.

Section III. The Comfort of Christ's Sufferings.

12. Until the present we have been in the Passion week and have celebrated Good Friday in the right way: now we come to Easter and Christ's resurrection. When man perceives his sins in this light and is completely terror-stricken in his conscience, he must be on his guard that his sins do not thus remain in his conscience, and nothing but pure doubt certainly come out of it; but just as the sins flowed out of Christ and we became conscious of them, so should we pour them again upon him and set our conscience free. Therefore see well to it that you act not like perverted people, who bite and devour themselves with their sins in their heart, and run here and there with their good works or their own satisfaction, or even work themselves out of this condition by means of indulgences and become rid of their sins; which is impossible, and, alas, such a false refuge of satisfaction and pilgrimages has spread far and wide.

13. Thirteenthly. Then cast your sins from yourself upon Christ, believe with a festive spirit that your sins are his wounds and sufferings, that he carries them and makes satisfaction for them, as Is 53:6 says: "Jehovah hath laid on him the iniquity of us all;" and St. Peter in his first Epistle 2:24: "Who his own

self bare our sins in his body upon the tree" of the cross; and St. Paul in 2 Cor. 5:21: "Him who knew no sin was made to be sin on our behalf; that we might become the righteousness of God in him." Upon these and like passages you must rely with all your weight, and so much the more the harder your conscience martyrs you. For if you do not take this course, but miss the opportunity of stilling your heart, then you will never secure peace, and must yet finally despair in doubt. For if we deal with our sins in our conscience and let them continue within us and be cherished in our hearts, they become much too strong for us to manage and they will live forever. But when we see that they are laid on Christ and he has triumphed over them by his resurrection and we fearlessly believe it, then they are dead and have become as nothing. For upon Christ they cannot rest, there they are swallowed up by his resurrection, and you see now no wound, no pain, in him, that is, no sign of sin. Thus St. Paul speaks in Rom. 4:25, that he was delivered up for our trespasses and was raised for our justification; that is, in his sufferings he made known our sins and also crucified them; but by his resurrection he makes us righteous and free from all sin, even if we believe the same differently.

14. Fourteenthly. Now if you are not able to believe, then, as I said before, you should pray to God for faith. For this is a matter in the hands of God that is entirely free, and is also bestowed alike at times knowingly, at times secretly, as was just said on the subject of suffering.

15. But now bestir yourself to the end: first, not to behold Christ's sufferings any longer; for they have already done their work and terrified you; but press through all difficulties and behold his friendly heart, how full of love it is toward you, which love constrained him to bear the heavy load of your conscience and your sin. Thus will your heart be loving and sweet toward him, and the assurance of your faith be strengthened. Then ascend higher through the heart of Christ to the heart of God, and see that Christ would not have been able to love you if God had not willed it in eternal love, to which Christ is obedient in his love toward you; there you will find the divine, good father heart, and, as Christ says, be thus drawn to the Father through Christ. Then will you understand the saying of Christ in Jn. 3:16: "God so loved the world that he gave his only begotten Son," etc. That means to know God aright, if we apprehend him not by his power and wisdom, which terrify us, but by his goodness and love; there our faith and confidence can then stand unmovable and man is truly thus born anew in God.

16. Sixteenthly. When your heart is thus established in Christ, and you are an enemy of sin, out of love and not out of fear of punishment, Christ's sufferings should also be an example for your whole life, and you should meditate on the same in a different way. For hitherto we have considered Christ's Passion as a sacrament that works in us and we suffer; now we consider it, that we also work, namely thus: if a day of sorrow or sickness weighs you down, think, how trifling that is, compared with the thorns and

nails of Christ. If you must do or leave undone what is distasteful to you: think, how Christ was led hither and thither, bound and a captive. Does pride attack you: behold, how your Lord was mocked and disgraced with murderers. Do unchastity and lust thrust themselves against you: think, how bitter it was for Christ to have his tender flesh torn, pierced and beaten again and again. Do hatred and envy war against you, or do you seek vengeance: remember how Christ with many tears and cries prayed for you and all his enemies, who indeed had more reason to seek revenge. If trouble or whatever adversity of body or soul afflict you, strengthen your heart and say: Ah, why then should I not also suffer a little since my Lord sweat blood in the garden because of anxiety and grief? That would be a lazy, disgraceful servant who would wish to lie in his bed while his lord was compelled to battle with the pangs of death.

17. Behold, one can thus find in Christ strength and comfort against all vice and bad habits. That is the right observance of Christ's Passion, and that is the fruit of his suffering, and he who exercises himself thus in the same does better than by hearing the whole Passion or reading all masses. And they are called true Christians who incorporate the life and name of Christ into their own life, as St. Paul says in Gal 5:24: "And they that are of Christ Jesus have crucified the flesh with the passions and the lusts thereof." For Christ's Passion must be dealt with not in words and a show, but in our lives and in truth. Thus St. Paul admonishes us in Heb. 12:3: "For consider him that hath endured such gainsaying of sinners against himself, that ye wax not weary, fainting in your souls;" and St. Peter in his 1st Epistle 4:1: "As Christ suffered in the flesh, arm ye yourselves also with the same mind." But this kind of meditation is now out of use and very rare, although the Epistles of St. Paul and St. Peter are full of it. We have changed the essence into a mere show, and painted the meditation of Christ's sufferings only in letters and on walls.

Enemies of the Cross of Christ & the Christian's Citizenship in Heaven.

PHILIPPIANS 3:17-21: Brethren, join in imitating me, and mark those who so live as you have an example in us. For many, of whom I have often told you and now tell you even with tears, live as enemies of the cross of Christ. Their end is destruction, their god is the belly, and they glory in their shame, with minds set on earthly things. But our commonwealth is in heaven, and from it we await a Savior, the Lord Jesus Christ, who will change our lowly body to be like his glorious body, by the power which enables him even to subject all things to himself.

1. Paul immeasurably extols the Philippians for having made a good beginning in the holy Gospel and for having acquitted themselves commendably, like men in earnest, as manifest by their fruits of faith. The reason he shows this sincere and strong concern for them is his desire that they remain steadfast, not being led astray by false teachers among the roaming Jews. For at that time many Jews went about with the intent of perverting Paul's converts, pretending they taught something far better; while they drew the people away from Christ and back to the Law, for the purpose of establishing and extending their Jewish doctrines. Paul, contemplating with special interest and pleasure his Church of the Philippians, is moved by parental care to admonish them--lest they sometime be misled by such teachers--to hold steadily to what they have received, not seeking anything else and not imagining, like self-secure, besotted souls who allow themselves to be deceived by the devil--not imagining themselves perfect and with complete understanding in all things. In the verses just preceding our text he speaks of himself as having not yet attained to full knowledge.

Purity of Doctrine Enjoined.

2. He particularly admonishes them to follow him and to mark those ministers who walk as he does; also to shape their belief and conduct by the pattern they have received from him. Not only of himself does he make an example, but introduces them who similarly walk, several of whom he mentions in this letter to the Philippians. The individuals whom be bids them

observe and follow must have been persons of special eminence. But it is particularly the doctrine the apostle would have the Philippians pattern after. Therefore we should be chiefly concerned about preserving the purity of the office of the ministry and the genuineness of faith. When these are kept unsullied, doctrine will be right, and good works spontaneous. Later on, in chapter 4, verse 8, Paul admonishes, with reference to the same subject: "If there be any virtue, and if there be any praise, think on these things."

3. Apparently Paul is a rash man to dare boast himself a pattern for all. Other ministers might well accuse him of desiring to exalt his individual self above others. "Think you," our wise ones would say to him, "that you alone have the Holy Spirit, or that no one else is as eager for honor as yourself?" Just so did Miriam and Aaron murmur against Moses, their own brother, saying: "Hath Jehovah indeed spoken only with Moses, hath he not spoken also with us?" (Num. 12:2). And it would seem as if Paul had too high an appreciation of his own character did he hold up his individual self as a pattern, intimating that no one was to be noted as worthy unless he walked as he did; though there might be some who apparently gave greater evidence of the Spirit, of holiness, humility and other graces, than himself, and yet walked not in his way.

4. But he does not say "I, Paul, alone." He says, "as ye have us for an example," that does not exclude other true apostles and teachers. He is admonishing his Church, as he everywhere does, to hold fast to the one true doctrine received from him in the beginning. They are not to be too confident of their own wisdom in the matter, or to presume they have independent authority; but rather to guard against pretenders to a superior doctrine, for so had some been misled.

Righteousness of the Law Is Vain.

5. In what respect he was a pattern or example to them, he has made plain; for instance, in the beginning of this chapter, in the third verse and following, he says: "For we are the circumcision, who worship by the Spirit of God, and glory in Christ Jesus, and have no confidence in the flesh: though I myself might have confidence even in the flesh: if any other man thinketh to have confidence in the flesh, I yet more: circumcised the eighth day, of the stock of Israel, of the tribe of Benjamin, a Hebrew of Hebrews." That is, he commands the highest honor a Jew can boast. "As touching the law," he goes on, "a Pharisee; as touching zeal, persecuting the Church, as touching the righteousness which is in the law, found blameless. Howbeit what things were gain to me, these have I counted loss for Christ. Yea verily, and I count all things to be loss for the excellency of the knowledge of Christ Jesus my Lord: for who I suffered the loss of all things, and do count them but refuse, that I may gain Christ, and be found in him, not having a righteousness of mine own, even that which is of the law, but that which is through faith in Christ, the righteousness which is from God by faith."

6. "Behold, this is the picture or pattern," he would say, "which we hold up for you to follow, that remembering how you obtained righteousness you may hold to it--a righteousness not of the Law." So far as the righteousness of the Law is concerned, Paul dares to say he regards it as filth and refuse (that proceeds from the human body); notwithstanding in its beautiful and blameless form it may be unsurpassed by anything in the world--such righteousness as was manifest in sincere Jews, and in Paul himself before his conversion; for these in their great holiness, regarded Christians as knaves and meriting damnation, and consequently took delight in being party to the persecution and murder of Christians.

7. "Yet," Paul would say, "I who am a Jew by birth have counted all this merit as simply loss that I might be found in 'the righteousness which is from God by faith.'" Only the righteousness of faith teaches us how to apprehend God--how to confidently console ourselves with his grace and await a future life, expecting to approach Christ in the resurrection. By "approaching" him we mean to meet him in death and at the judgment day without terror, not fleeing but gladly drawing near and hailing him with joy as one waited for with intense longing.

Now, the righteousness of the Law cannot effect such confidence of mind. Hence, for me it avails nothing before God; rather it is a detriment. What does avail is God's imputation of righteousness for Christ's sake, through faith. God declares to us in his Word that the believer in his Son shall, for Christ's own sake, have God's grace and eternal life. He who knows this is able to wait in hope for the last day, having no fear, no disposition to flee.

8. But is it not treating the righteousness of the Law with irreverence and contempt to regard it--and so teach as something not only useless and even obstructive, but injurious, loathsome and abominable? Who would have been able to make such a bold statement, and to censure a life so faultless and conforming so closely to the Law as Paul's, without being pronounced by all men a minion of the devil, had not the apostle made that estimation of it himself? And who is to have any more respect for the righteousness of the Law if we are to preach in that strain?

9. Had Paul confined his denunciations to the righteousness of the world or of the heathen--the righteousness dependent upon reason and controlled by secular government, by laws and regulations--his teaching would not have seemed so irreverent. But he distinctly specifies the righteousness of God's Law, or the Ten Commandments, to which we owe an obligation far above what is due temporal powers, for they teach how to live before God--something no heathenish court of justice, no temporal authority, knows anything about. Should we not condemn as a heretic this preacher who goes beyond his prerogative and dares find fault with the Law of God? who also warns us to shun such as observe it, such as trust in its righteousness, and exalts to

sainthood "enemies of the cross of Christ whose God is the belly"--who serve the appetites instead of God?

10. Paul would say of himself: "I, too, was such a one. In my most perfect righteousness of the Law I was an enemy to and persecutor of the congregation, or Church, of Christ. It was the legitimate fruit of my righteousness that I though I must be party to the most horrible persecution of Christ and his Christians. Thus my holiness made me an actual enemy of Christ and a murderer of his followers. The disposition to injure is a natural result of the righteousness of the Law, as all Scripture history from Cain down testifies, and as we see even in the best of the world who have not come to the knowledge of Christ. Princes, civil authorities in proportion to their wisdom, their godliness and honor are the bitter and intolerant enemies of the Gospel.

11. Of the sensual papistical dolts at Rome, cardinals, bishops, priests and the like, it is not necessary to speak here. Their works are manifest. All honorable secular authorities must confess they are simply abandoned knaves, living shameless lives of open scandal, avarice, arrogance, unchastity, vanity, robbery and wickedness of every kind. Not only are they guilty of such living, but shamelessly endeavor to defend their conduct. They must, then, be regarded enemies of Christ and of all honesty and virtue. Hence every respectable man is justly antagonistic toward them. But, as before said, Paul is not here referring to this class, but to eminent, godly individuals, whose lives are beyond reproach. These very ones, when Christians are encountered, are hostile and heinous enough to be able to forget all their own faults in the sight of God, and to magnify to huge beams the motes we Christians have. In fact, they must style the Gospel heresy and satanic doctrine for the purpose of exalting their own holiness and zeal for God.

Righteousness of the Law Opposes the Cross.

12. The thing seems incredible, and I would not have believed it myself, nor have understood Paul's words here, had I not witnessed it with my own eyes and experienced it. Were the apostle to repeat the charge today, who could conceive that our first, noblest, most respectable, godly and holy people, those whom we might expect, above all others, to accept the Word of God--that they, I say, should be enemies to the Christian doctrine? But the examples before us testify very plainly that the "enemies" the apostle refers to must be the individuals styled godly and worthy princes and noblemen, honorable citizens, learned, wise, intelligent individuals. Yet if these could devour at one bite the "Evangelicals," as they are now called, they would do it.

13. If you ask, Whence such a disposition? I answer, it naturally springs from human righteousness. For every individual who professes human righteousness, and knows nothing of Christ, holds that efficacious before God. He relies upon it and gratifies himself with it, presuming thereby to present a flattering appearance in God's sight and to render himself peculiarly acceptable

to him. From being proud and arrogant toward God, he comes to reject them who are not righteous according to the Law; as illustrated in the instance of the Pharisee (Lk. 18:11-12). But greater is his enmity and more bitter his hatred toward the preaching that dares to censure such righteousness and assert its futility to merit God's grace and eternal life.

14. I myself, and others with me, were dominated by such feelings when, under popery, we claimed to be holy and pious; we must confess the fact. If thirty years ago, when I was a devout, holy monk, holding mass every day and having no thought but that I was in the road leading directly to heaven--if then anyone had accused me--had preached to me the things of this text and pronounced our righteousness--which accorded not strictly with the Law of God, but conformed to human doctrine and was manifestly idolatrous--pronounced it without efficacy and said I was an enemy to the cross of Christ, serving my own sensual appetites, I would immediately have at least helped to find stones for putting to death such a Stephen, or to gather wood for the burning of this worst of heretics.

15. So human nature ever does. The world cannot conduct itself in any other way, when the declaration comes from heaven saying: "True you are a holy man, a great and learned jurist, a conscientious regent, a worthy prince, an honorable citizen, and so on, but with all your authority and your upright character you are going to hell; your every act is offensive and condemned in God's sight. If you would be saved you must become an altogether different man; your mind and heart must be changed." Let this be announced and the fire rises, the Rhine is all ablaze; for the self-righteous regard it an intolerable idea that lives so beautiful, lives devoted to praiseworthy callings, should be publicly censured and condemned by the objectionable preaching of a few insignificant individuals regarded as even pernicious, and according to Paul, as filthy refuse, actual obstacles to eternal life.

16. But you may say: "What? Do you forbid good works? Is it not right to lead an honorable, virtuous life? Do you not acknowledge the necessity of political laws, of civil governments? that upon obedience to them depends the maintenance of discipline, peace and honor? Indeed, do you not admit that God himself commands such institutions and wills their observance, punishing where they are disregarded? Much more would he have his own Law and the Ten Commandments honored, not rejected. How dare you then assert that such righteousness is misleading, and obstructive to eternal life? What consistence is there in teaching people to observe the things of the Law, to be righteous in that respect, and at the same time censuring those things as condemned before God? How can the works of the Law be good and precious, and yet repulsive and productive of evil?"

17. I answer, Paul well knows the world takes its stand on this point of righteousness by the Law, and hence would contradict him. But let him who will, consult the apostle as to why he makes such bold assertions here. For

indeed the words of the text are not our words, but his. True, law and government are essential in temporal life, as Paul himself confesses, and God would have everyone honor and obey them. Indeed, he has ordained their observance among Turks and heathen. Yet it is a fact that these people, even the best and most upright of them, they who lead honorable lives, are naturally in their hearts enemies to Christ, and devote their intellectual powers to exterminating God's people.

It must be universally admitted that the Turks, with all the restrictions and austerity of life imposed upon them by the Koran, a life more rigorous even than that of Christians--it must be admitted they belong to the devil. In other words, we adjudge them condemned with all their righteousness, but at the same time say they do right in punishing thieves, robbers, murderers, drunkards and other offenders; more, that Christians living within their jurisdiction are under obligation to pay tribute, and to serve them with person and property. Precisely the same thing is true respecting our princes who persecute the Gospel and are open enemies to Christ: we must be obedient to them, paying the tribute and rendering the service imposed; yet they, and all obedient followers willingly consenting to the persecution of the Gospel, must be looked upon as condemned before God.

18. Similarly does Paul speak concerning the righteousness of all the Jews and pious saints who are not Christians. His utterance is bold and of certain sound. He censures them and, weeping, deprecatingly refers to certain who direct the people to the righteousness of the law with the sole result of making "enemies to the cross of Christ."

19. Again, all the praise he has for them is to say that their "end is perdition"; they are condemned in spite of strenuous efforts all their lives to teach and enforce the righteousness of works. Here on earth it is truly a priceless distinction, an admirable and noble treasure, a praiseworthy honor, to have the name of being a godly and upright prince, ruler or citizen; a pious, virtuous wife or virgin. Who would not praise and exalt such virtue? It is indeed a rare and valuable thing in the world. But however beautiful, priceless and admirable an honor it is, Paul tells us, it is ultimately condemned and pertains not to heaven.

Human Righteousness Idolatrous.

20. The apostle makes his accusation yet more galling with the words "whose god is their belly." Thus you hear how human righteousness, even at its best, extends no higher than to service of the sensual appetites. Take all the wisdom, justice, jurisprudence, artifice, even the highest virtues the world affords, and what are they? They minister only to that god, carnal appetite. They can go no farther than the needs of this life, their whole purpose being to satisfy physical cravings. When the physical appetites of the worldly pass, they pass likewise, and the gifts and virtues we have mentioned can no longer serve

them. All perish and go to destruction together--righteousness, virtues, laws and physical appetites which they have served as their god. For they are wholly ignorant of the true and eternal God; they know not how to serve him and receive eternal life. So then in its essential features such a life is merely idolatrous, having no greater object than the preservation of this perishable body and its enjoyment of peace and honor.

21. The fourth accusation is, "whose glory is in their shame." That is all their glory amounts to. Let wise philosophers, scrupulous heathen, keen jurists, receive the acme of praise and honor--it is yet but shame. True, their motto is "Love of Virtue"; they boast strong love of virtue and righteousness and may even think themselves sincere. But judged by final results, their boast is without foundation and ends in shame. For the utmost their righteousness can effect is the applause of the world--here on earth. Before God it avails nothing. It cannot touch the life to come. Ultimately it leaves its possessor a captive in shame. Death devours and hell clutches him.

22. You may again object, "If what you say it true, why observe temporal restrictions? Let us live in indulgent carelessness following our inclinations. Let pass the godly, honorable man; the virtuous, upright wife or virgin." I answer, By no means; that is not the design. You have heard it is God's command and will that there be temporal righteousness even among Turks and heathen. And later on (ch. 4, 8) Paul admonishes Christians to "think on these things," that is, on what is true. He says: "Whatsoever things are honorable, whatsoever things are just, whatsoever things are pure, whatsoever things are lovely, whatsoever things are of good report; if there be any virtue, and if there be any praise, think on these things." And continuing, in verse 9, he refers them to his own example, saying, "which ye both learned and received and heard and saw in me."

Fruits of Faith.

23. With the believers in Christ, them who have their righteousness in him, there should follow in this life on earth the fruits of upright living, in obedience to God. These fruits constitute the good works acceptable to God, which, being works of faith and wrought in Christ, will be rewarded in the life to come. But Paul has in mind the individuals who, rejecting faith in Christ, regard their self-directed lives, their humanly-wrought works, which conform to the Law, as righteousness availing in the sight of God. His reference is to them who so trust, though wholly ignorant of Christ, for whose sake, without any merit on our part, righteousness is imputed to us by God. The only condition is we must believe in Christ; for he became man, died for our sins and rose from the dead, for the very purpose of liberating us from our sins and granting us his resurrection and life. Toward the heavenly life we should tend, in our life here walking in harmony with it; as Paul says in conclusion: "Our citizenship is in heaven [not earthly and not confined to this temporal life only]; whence also we

wait for a Saviour, the Lord Jesus Christ."

If we have no knowledge, no consciousness, of this fact, it matters not how beautiful and praiseworthy our human, earthly righteousness may be, it is merely a hindrance and an injury. For flesh and blood cannot help relying on its own righteousness and arrogantly boasting in this strain: "We are better, more honorable, more godly, than others. We Jews are the people of God and keep his Law." Even Christians are not wholly free from the pernicious influence of human holiness. They ever seek to bring their own works and merits before God. I know for myself what pains are inflicted by this godless wisdom, this figment of righteousness, and what effort must be made before the serpent's head is bruised.

24. Now, this is the situation and there is no alternative: Either suffer hell or regard your human righteousness as loss and filth and endeavor not to be found relying on it at your last hour, in the presence of God and judgment, but rather stand in the righteousness of Christ. In the garment of Christ's righteousness and reared in him you may, in the resurrection from sin and death, meet Christ and exclaim: "Hail, beloved Lord and Saviour, thou who hast redeemed me from the wretched body of sin and death, and fashioned me like unto thy holy, pure and glorious body!"

God's Patience with Human Righteousness.

25. Meantime, while we walk in the faith of his righteousness, he has patience with the poor, frail righteousness of this earthly life, which otherwise is but filth in his sight. He honors our human holiness by supporting and protecting it during the time we live on earth; just as we honor our corrupt, filthy bodies, adorning them with beautiful,costly garments and golden ornaments, and reposing them on cushions and beds of luxury. Though but stench and filth encased in flesh, they are honored above everything else on earth. For their sake are all things performed--the ordering and ruling, building and laboring; and God himself permits sun and moon to shine that they may receive light and heat, and everything to grow on earth for their benefit. What is the human body but a beautiful pyx containing that filthy, repulsive object of reverence, the digestive organs, which the body must always patiently carry about; yes, which we must even nourish and minister to, glad if only they perform their functions properly?

26. Similarly God deals with us. Because he would confer eternal life upon man, he patiently endures the filthy righteousness of this life wherein we must dwell until the last day, for the sake of his chosen people and until the number is complete. For so long as the final day is deferred, not all to have eternal life are yet born. When the time shall be fulfilled, the number completed, God will suddenly bring to an end the world with its governments, its jurists and authorities, its conditions of life; in short, he will utterly abolish earthly righteousness, destroying physical appetites and all else together. For every

form of human holiness is condemned to destruction; yet for the sake of Christians, to whom eternal life is appointed, and for their sake only, all these must be perpetuated until the last saint is born and has attained life everlasting. Were there but one saint yet to be born, for the sake of that one the world must remain. For God regards not the world nor has he need for it, except for the sake of his Christians.

27. Therefore, when God enjoins upon us obedience to the emperor, and godly, honest lives on earth, it is no warrant that our subjection to temporal authority is to continue forever. Instead, God necessarily will minister to, adorn and honor this wretched body--vile body, as Paul here has it--with power and dominion. Yet the apostle terms human righteousness "filth," and says it is not necessary to God's kingdom; indeed, that it is condemned in the sight of God with all its honor and glory, and all the world must be ashamed of it in his presence, confessing themselves guilty. Paul in Romans 3:27 and 4:2 testifies to this fact when he tells how even the exalted, holy fathers--Abraham, and others--though having glory before the world because of their righteous works, could not make them serve to obtain honor before God. Much less will worldly honor avail with God in the case of individuals who, being called honorable, pious, honest, virtuous--lords and princes, wives and husbands--boast of such righteousness.

28. Outwardly, then, though your righteousness may appear dazzlingly beautiful before the world, inwardly you are but filth. Illustrative of this point is the story told of a certain nun regarded holy above all others. She would not fellowship with anyone else, but sat alone in her cell in wrapt devotion, praying unceasingly. She boasted special revelations and visions and had no consciousness of anything but that beloved angels hovered about and adorned her with a golden crown. But some outside, ardently desiring to behold such sights, peeped through holes and crevices, and seeing her head but defiled with filth, laughed at her.

29. Notice, the reason Paul calls the righteousness of the Law filth and pollution, is his desire to denounce the honor and glory claimed for it in God's sight; notwithstanding he honors before the world the observance of the Law by styling it "righteousness." But if you ostentatiously boast of such righteousness to him, he pronounces his sentence of judgment making you an abomination, an enemy of the cross of Christ, and shaming your boasted honor and finally casting you into hell. Concerning the righteousness of faith, however, which in Christ avails before God, he says: "Our citizenship [conversation] is in heaven, from whence also we look for the Saviour, the Lord Jesus Christ; who shall change our vile body, that it may be fashioned like unto his glorious body."

30. We who are baptized and believe in Christ, Paul's thought is, do not base our works and our hope on the righteouness of this temporal life. Through faith in Christ, we have a righteousness that holds in heaven. It abides in Christ

alone; otherwise it would avail naught before God. And our whole concern is to be eternally in Christ; to have our earthly existence culminate in yonder life when Christ shall come and change this life into another, altogether new, pure, holy and like unto his own, with a life and a body having the nature of his.

The Christian a Citizen of Heaven.

31. Therefore we are no longer citizens of earth. The baptized Christian is born a citizen of heaven through baptism. We should be mindful of this fact and walk here as if native there. We are to console ourselves with the fact that God thus accepts us and will transplant us there. Meantime we must await the coming again of the Saviour, who is to bring from heaven to us eternal righteousness, life, honor and glory.

32. We are baptized and made Christians, not to the end that we may have great honor, or renown of righteousness, or earthly dominion, power and possessions. Notwithstanding we do have these because they are requisite to our physical life, yet we are to regard them as mere filth, wherewith we minister to our bodily welfare as best we can for the benefit of posterity. We Christians, however, are expectantly to await the coming of the Saviour. His coming will not be to our injury or shame as it may be in the case of others. He comes for the salvation of our unprofitable, impotent bodies. Wretchedly worthless as they are in this life, they are much more unprofitable when lifeless and perishing in the earth.

33. But, however miserable, powerless and contemptible in life and death, Christ will at his coming render our bodies beautiful, pure, shining and worthy of honor, until they correspond to his own immortal, glorious body. Not like it as it hung on the cross or lay in the grave, bloodstained, livid and disgraced; but as it is now, glorified at the Father's right hand. We need not, then, be alarmed at the necessity of laying aside our earthly bodies; at being despoiled of the honor, righteousness and life adhering in them, to deliver it to the devouring power of death and the grave--something well calculated to terrify the enemies of Christ: but we may joyfully hope for and await his speedy coming to deliver us from this miserable, filthy pollution.

"According to the working whereby he is able even to subdue all things unto himself."

The Glorified Body of the Christian.

34. Think of the honor and the glory Christ's righteousness brings even to our bodies! How can this poor, sinful, miserable, filthy, polluted body become like unto that of the Son of God, the Lord of Glory? What are you--your powers and abilities, or those of all men, to effect this glorious thing? But Paul says human righteousness, merit, glory and power have nothing to do with it. They are mere filth and pollution, and condemned as well. Another force intervenes,

the power of Christ the Lord, who is able to bring all things into subjection to himself. Now, if he has power to subject all things unto himself at will, he is also able to glorify the pollution and filth of this wretched body, even when it has become worms and dust. In his hands it is as clay in the hands of the potter, and from the polluted lump of clay he can make a vessel that shall be a beautiful, new, pure, glorious body, surpassing the sun in its brilliance and beauty.

35. Through baptism Christ has taken us into his hands, actually that he may exchange our sinful, condemned, perishable, physical lives for the new, imperishable righteousness and life he prepares for body and soul. Such is the power and the agency exalting us to marvelous glory--something no earthly righteousness of the Law could accomplish. The righteousness of the Law leaves our bodies to shame and destruction; it reaches not beyond physical existence. But the righteousness of Christ inspires with power, making evident that we worship not the body but the true and living God, who does not leave us to shame and destruction, but delivers from sin, death and condemnation, and exalts this perishable body to eternal honor and glory.

Christ Our Great High Priest

HEBREWS 9:11-15: But Christ being come an high priest of good things to come, by a greater and more perfect tabernacle, not made with hands, that is to say, not of this building; Neither by the blood of goats and calves, but by his own blood he entered in once into the holy place, having obtained eternal redemption for us. For if the blood of bulls and of goats, and the ashes of an heifer sprinkling the unclean, sanctifieth to the purifying of the flesh: How much more shall the blood of Christ, who through the eternal Spirit offered himself without spot to God, purge your conscience from dead works to serve the living God? And for this cause he is the mediator of the new testament, that by means of death, for the redemption of the transgressions that were under the first testament, they which are called might receive the promise of eternal inheritance.

1. An understanding of practically all of the Epistle to the Hebrews is necessary before we can hope to make this text clear to ourselves. Briefly, the epistle treats of a twofold priesthood. The former priesthood was a material one, with material adornment, tabernacle, sacrifices and with pardon couched in ritual; material were all its appointments. The new order is a spiritual priesthood, with spiritual adornments, spiritual tabernacle and sacrifices--spiritual in all that pertains to it. Christ, in the exercise of his priestly office, in the sacrifice on the cross, was not adorned with silk and gold and precious stones, but with divine love, wisdom, patience, obedience and all virtues. His adornment was apparent to none but God and possessors, of the Spirit, for it was spiritual.

2. Christ sacrificed not goats nor calves nor birds; not bread; not blood nor flesh, as did Aaron and his posterity: he offered his own body and blood, and the manner of the sacrifice was spiritual; for it took place through the Holy Spirit, as here stated. Though the body and blood of Christ were visible the same as any other material object, the fact that he offered them as a sacrifice was not apparent. It was not a visible sacrifice, as in the case of offerings at the hands of Aaron. Then the goat or calf, the flesh and blood, were material sacrifices visibly offered, and recognized as sacrifices. But Christ offered himself in the heart before God. His sacrifice was perceptible to no mortal. Therefore, his bodily flesh and blood becomes a spiritual sacrifice. Similarly, we Christians,

the posterity of Christ our Aaron, offer up our own bodies (Rom 12:1). And our offering is likewise a spiritual sacrifice, or, as Paul has it, a "reasonable service"; for we make it in spirit, and it is beheld of God alone.

3. Again, in the new order, the tabernacle or house is spiritual; for it is heaven, or the presence of God. Christ hung upon a cross; he was not offered in a temple. He was offered before the eyes of God, and there he still abides. The cross is an altar in a spiritual sense. The material cross was indeed visible, but none knew it as Christ's altar. Again, his prayer, his sprinkled blood, his burnt incense, were all spiritual, for it was all wrought through his spirit.

4. Accordingly, the fruit and blessing of his office and sacrifice, the forgiveness of our sins and our justification, are likewise spiritual. In the Old Covenant, the priest with his sacrifices and sprinklings of blood effected merely as it were an external absolution, or pardon, corresponding to the childhood stage of the people. The recipient was permitted to move publicly among the people; he was externally holy and as one restored from excommunication. He who failed to obtain absolution from the priest was unholy, being denied membership in the congregation and enjoyment of its privileges; in all respects he was separated like those in the ban today.

5. But such absolution rendered no one inwardly holy and just before God. Something beyond that was necessary to secure true forgiveness. It was the same principle which governs church discipline today. He who has received no more than the remission, or absolution, of the ecclesiastical judge will surely remain forever out of heaven. On the other hand, he who is in the ban of the Church is hellward bound only when the sentence is confirmed at a higher tribunal. I can make no better comparison than to say that it was the same in the old Jewish priesthood as now in the Papal priesthood, which, with its loosing and binding, can prohibit or permit only external communion among Christians. It is true, God required such measures in the time of the Jewish dispensation, that he might restrain by fear; just as now he sanctions church discipline when rightly employed, in order to punish and restrain the evil-doer, though it has no power in itself to raise people to holiness or to push them into wickedness.

6. But with the priesthood of Christ is true spiritual remission, sanctification and absolution. These avail before God--God grant that it be true of us--whether we be outwardly excommunicated, or holy, or not. Christ's blood has obtained for us pardon forever acceptable with God. God will forgive our sins for the sake of that blood so long as its power shall last and its intercession for grace in our behalf, which is forever. Therefore, we are forever holy and blessed before God. This is the substance of the text. Now that we shall find it easy to understand, we will briefly consider it.

"But Christ having come a high priest of the good things to come."

7. The adornment of Aaron and his descendants, the high priests, was of a material nature, and they obtained for the people a merely formal remission of

sins, performing their office in a perishable temple, or tabernacle. It was evident to men that their absolution and sanctification before the congregation was a temporal blessing confined to the present. But when Christ came upon the cross no one beheld him as he went before God in the Holy Spirit, adorned with every grace and virtue, a true High Priest. The blessings wrought by him are not temporal--a merely formal pardon--but the "blessings to come"; namely, blessings which are spiritual and eternal. Paul speaks of them as blessings to come, not that we are to await the life to come before we can have forgiveness and all the blessings of divine grace, but because now we possess them only in faith. They are as yet hidden, to be revealed in the future life. Again, the blessings we have in Christ were, from the standpoint of the Old Testament priesthood, blessings to come.

"Through the greater and more perfect tabernacle, not made with hands, that is to say, not of this creation.

8. The apostle does not name the tabernacle he mentions; nor can he, so strange its nature! It exists only in the sight of God, and is ours in faith, to be revealed hereafter. It is not made with hands, like the Jewish tabernacle; in other words, not of "this building." The old tabernacle, like all buildings of its nature, necessarily was made of wood and other temporal materials created by God. God says in Isaiah 66:1-2: "What manner of house will ye build unto me?....For all these things hath my hand made, and so all these things came to be." But that greater tabernacle has not yet form; it is not yet finished. God is building it and he shall reveal it. Christ's words are (Jn. 14:3), "And if I go and prepare a place for you."

"Nor yet through the blood of goats and calves, but through his own blood, entered in once for all into the holy place, having obtained eternal redemption."

9. According to Leviticus 16, the high priest must once a year enter into the holy place with the blood of rams and other offerings, and with these make formal reconciliation for the people. This ceremony typified that Christ, the true Priest, should once die for us, to obtain for us the true atonement. But the former sacrifice, having to be repeated every year, was but a temporary and imperfect atonement; it did not eternally suffice, as does the atonement of Christ. For though we fall and sin repeatedly, we have confidence that the blood of Christ does not fall, or sin; it remains steadfast before God, and the expiation is perpetual and eternal. Under its sway grace is perpetually renewed, without work or merit on our part, provided we do not stand aloof in unbelief.

"For if the blood of goats and bulls, and the ashes of a heifer," etc.

10. Concerning the water of separation and the ashes of the red heifer, read Numbers 19; and concerning the blood of bulls and goats, Leviticus 16:14-15. According to Paul, these were formal and temporal purifications, as I stated above. But Christ, in God's sight, purifies the conscience of dead works; that is, of sins meriting death, and of works performed in sin and therefore dead. Christ purifies from these, that we may serve the living God by living works.

"And for this cause he is the mediator of a new covenant [testament]," etc.

11. Under the old law, which provided only for formal, or ritualistic pardon, and restored to human fellowship, sin and transgressions remained, burdening the conscience. It--the old law--did not benefit the soul at all, inasmuch as God did not institute it to purify and safeguard the conscience, nor to bestow the Spirit. It existed merely for the purpose of outward discipline, restraint and correction. So Paul teaches that under the Old Testament dispensation man's transgressions remained, but now Christ is our Mediator through his blood; by it our conscience, is freed from sin in the sight of God, inasmuch as God promises the Spirit through the blood of Christ. All, however, do not receive him. Only those called to be heirs eternal, the elect, receive the Spirit.

12. We find, then, in this excellent lesson, the comforting doctrine taught that Christ is he whom we should know as the Priest and Bishop of our souls; that no sin is forgiven, nor the Holy Spirit given, by reason of works or merit on our part, but alone through the blood of Christ, and that to those for whom God has ordained it. This matter has been sufficiently set forth in the various postils.

On Faith & Coming to Christ

On Faith and Coming to Christ, and the True Bread of Heaven:

JOHN 6:44-55: No man can come to me, except the Father which hath sent me draw him: and I will raise him up at the last day. It is written in the prophets, And they shall be all taught of God. Every man therefore that hath heard, and hath learned of the Father, cometh unto me. Not that any man hath seen the Father, save he which is of God, he hath seen the Father. Verily, verily, I say unto you, He that believeth on me hath everlasting life. I am that bread of life. Your fathers did eat manna in the wilderness, and are dead. This is the bread which cometh down from heaven, that a man may eat thereof, and not die. I am the living bread which came down from heaven: if any man eat of this bread, he shall live for ever: and the bread that I will give is my flesh, which I will give for the life of the world. The Jews therefore strove among themselves, saying, How can this man give us his flesh to eat? Then Jesus said unto them, Verily, verily, I say unto you, Except ye eat the flesh of the Son of man, and drink his blood, ye have no life in you. Whoso eateth my flesh, and drinketh my blood, hath eternal life; and I will raise him up at the last day. For my flesh is meat indeed, and my blood is drink indeed.

Section I. On Faith, and Coming to Christ.

1. This Gospel text teaches exclusively of the Christian faith, and awakens that faith in us; just as John, throughout his whole Gospel, simply instructs us how to trust in Christ the Lord. This faith alone, when based upon the sure promises of God, must save us; as our text clearly explains. And in the light of it all, they must become fools who have taught us other ways to become godly.

All that human ingenuity can devise, be it as holy and as luminous as it may, must tumble to the ground if man be saved in God's way--in a way different from that which man himself plans. Man may forever do as he will, he can never enter heaven unless God takes the first step with his Word, which offers him divine grace and enlightens his heart so as to get upon the right way.

2. This right way, however, is the Lord Jesus Christ. Whoever desires to seek another way, as the great multitudes venture to do by means of their own works, has already missed the right way; for Paul says to the Galatians: "If righteousness is through the Law," that is, through the works of the Law, "then Christ died for naught" (Gal. 2:21). Therefore I say man must fall upon this Gospel and be broken to pieces and in deep consciousness lie prostrate, like a man that is powerless, unable to move hand or foot. He must only lie motionless and cry: Almighty God, merciful Father, now help me! I cannot help myself. Christ, my Lord, do help now, for with only my own effort all is lost! Thus, in the light of this cornerstone, which is Christ, everyone becomes as nothing; as Christ says of himself in Luke 20:17-18, when he asks the Pharisees and scribes: "What then is this that is written. The stone which the builders rejected, the same was made the head of the corner? Every one that falleth on that stone shall be 'broken to pieces; but on whomsoever it shall fall, it will scatter him as dust" (Ps. 118:22). Therefore, we must either fall upon this stone, Christ, in all our inability and helplessness, rejecting our own merits, and be broken to pieces, or he will forever crush us by his severe sentence and judgment. It is better that we fall upon him than that he should fall upon us. For this reason the Lord says in this Gospel: "No man can come to me, except the Father that sent me draw him: and I will raise him up in the last day."

3. He must surely perish whom the rather does not draw. Thus it is decreed, that whoever does not come to this Son must be condemned forever. The Son is given to us only to the end that he may save us; besides him, nothing saves us, either in heaven or on earth. If he does not help us, then nothing will. On this Peter says in the Acts of the Apostles (4:11-12): "He is the stone which was set at naught of you the builders, which was made the head of the corner. And in none other is there salvation; neither is there any other name underheaven, that is given among men, wherein we must be saved." Where, in the light of this, are our theologians and professors who taught us that we become pious through our many good works? Here the great master Aristotle is put to shame, who proclaimed that reason strives for the best and always follows after the good. Christ says to this: No; if the rather comes not first and draws men, they must forever perish.

4. Here all men must confess their incapacity and inability to do the good. Should one imagine he is able to do anything good of his own strength he does no less than make Christ the Lord a liar; he would rudely and defiantly come to the Father and in all rashness ascend to heaven. Therefore, where the pure and plain Word of God goes, it breaks into pieces everything that is exalted of

man, it makes valleys of all their mountains, and all their hills it makes low, as the prophet Isaiah (40:4) says. Every heart that hears this Word must lose faith in itself, else it will not be able to come to Christ. God's works do nothing but destroy and make alive, condemn and minister salvation. Hannah, the mother of Samuel, sings of the Lord: "Jehovah killeth, and maketh alive; he bringeth down to the grave and bringeth up" (1 Sam. 2:6).

5. Hence, a person who is thus smitten in his heart, by God, to confess that he is one who, on account of his sins, must be condemned, is like the righteous man whom with the first words of this Gospel God wounds, and because of that wound fixes upon him the band or cord of his divine grace, by which he draws him, so that he must seek help and counsel for his soul. Before he could not obtain any help or counsel from God, nor did he ever desire it; but now he finds the first comfort and promise of God, which Luke 2:10 records thus: "For every one that asketh receiveth; and he that seeketh findeth; and to him that knocketh it shall be opened." From such promises will he ever continue to gain courage as long as he lives, and will ever win greater and greater confidence in God. Just as soon as he hears that grace is the work of God alone, he will desire it of God as from the hand of his gracious Father, who wishes to draw him. Now, if he is drawn by God to Christ, he will certainly experience what the Lord here says: "He will raise him up in the last day." For he has laid hold upon the Word of God and trusts God. In this he has a sure sign that he is one whom God has drawn, as John says in his First Epistle (5:10): "He that believeth on the Son of God hath the witness in him."

6. Hence, it must necessarily follow that he is taught of God, and that he knows now in truth that the meaning of God is nothing more than Helper, Comforter, Saviour, as we say of those who rescue us from danger: Thou wast today my God. From this it is now clear that God will be to us nothing less than a saviour, a helper, and a giver of all blessedness, who neither demands nor desires anything from us. He only gives, he only offers to us; as he says to Israel in Ps. 81:10: "I am Jehovah thy God, who brought thee up out of the land of Egypt: open thy mouth wide, and I will fill it." Who would not be kindly disposed to such a God, who approaches us so lovingly and graciously, and offers us his favor and blessings if we only acknowledge him as God and are willing to be taught of him? They cannot escape the severe, eternal judgment of God who ignore such grace, as the Epistle to the Hebrews (10:28-29) says: "A man that hath set at naught Moses' law dieth without compassion: of how much sorer punishment, think ye, shall he be judged worthy, who hath trodden under foot the Son of God, and hath counted the blood of the covenant wherewith he was sanctified an unholy thing."

7. Oh, how diligent and earnest St. Paul is in all his Epistles that we may always grasp the knowledge of God aright! How often he expresses the wish for growth in the knowledge of God! As if he would say: If you only knew and understood what God is, then you would be already saved, then you would gain

love for him and do only those things well pleasing to him. Thus he says to the Colossians (1:9-12): "For this cause we also, since the day we heard it, do not cease to pray and make request for you, that ye may be filled with the knowledge of his will in all spiritual wisdom and understanding, to walk worthily of the Lord unto all pleasing, bearing fruit in every good work, and increasing in knowledge of God; strengthened with all power, according to the might of his glory, unto all patience and longsuffering with joy; giving thanks unto the Father, who made us meet to be partakers of the inheritance of the saints in light." And in Ps. 119:34 David says: "Give me understanding, and I shall keep thy Law; yea, I shall observe it with my whole heart."

8. Thus you learn from the first utterance in today's Gospel that this knowledge must come from God the Father; he must lay the first stone of the foundation in us, else we will never do anything. But this is accomplished in the following way: God sends us preachers, whom he has taught, to preach to us his will. First he instructs us that our entire lives and characters, however beautiful and holy they may be, are before him as nothing, yea, are as abomination, and displeasing; this is called a preaching of the Law. Then he offers us grace; that is, he tells us that he will not utterly condemn and reject us, but will receive us in his beloved Son, and not merely receive us, but make us heirs of his kingdom, lords over all that is in heaven and upon earth. This is called preaching grace or preaching the Gospel. But God is the origin of all; he first awakens preachers and constrains them to preach. This is the meaning of St. Paul's words when he says to the Romans: "So belief cometh of hearing, and hearing by the Word of Christ" (Rom. 10:17). This truth the words of the Lord in today's Gospel also declares, when Christ says: "It is written in the prophets, And they shall all be taught of God. Every one that hath heard from the Father, and hath learned, cometh unto me. Not that any man hath seen the Father, save he that is from God, he hath seen the Father."

9. Now, under the first preaching, the preaching of the Law, namely, that we with all our works are condemned, man is restless and fearful before God, and knows not what to do with his life and deeds. He suffers from an accusing and timid conscience, and if relief from some source were not to come quickly he would have to despair forever. Therefore, we must not long delay with the other preaching; we must preach the Gospel to him and lead him to Christ as the one whom the Father has given to us to be our mediator, that we should be saved solely through him, out of pure grace and mercy, without any works or merit on our part. The heart rejoices at this word and runs to such grace as a thirsty deer to the water. This longing David keenly experiences when he says in Ps. 42:1-2: "As the heart panteth after the water brooks, so panteth my soul after thee, O God, my soul thirsteth for God, for the living God."

10. Now, when one comes to Christ, that is, to his Gospel, he hears the personal voice of Christ the Lord, which confirms the knowledge God taught him, namely, that God is nothing but a very gracious Saviour, who wants to be

gracious and merciful to all who call upon him. Therefore, the Lord adds:

"Verily verily, I say unto you, He that believeth hath eternal life. I am the bread of life. Your fathers ate the manna in the wilderness, and they died. This is the bread that cometh down out of heaven, that a man may eat thereof, and not die. I am the living bread that came down out of heaven: if any man eat of this bread, he shall live forever: yea and the bread which I will give is my flesh, for the life of the world."

11. In these words the soul finds a well prepared table, at which it satisfies all hunger; for it knows for a certainty that he who speaks these words cannot lie. Therefore the soul falls upon the Word, clings to it, trusts in it, and also builds its dwelling-place in the strength of this well-prepared table. This is the feast for which the heavenly Father slayed his oxen and fatlings and invited us all to it.

SECTION II. The Bread Of Heaven.

12. The living bread, of which the Lord here speaks, is Christ himself, of whom we partake. If in our hearts we lay hold of only a morsel of this bread, we shall have forever enough and can never be separated from God. The partaking of this bread is nothing but faith in Christ our Lord, that he is, as Paul says in 1 Cor. 1:30, "made unto us wisdom from God, and righteousness and sanctification, and redemption." He who eats of this food lives forever. Therefore, the Lord says, immediately following this Gospel lesson, where the Jews strove among themselves about this discourse of his: "Verily, verily, I say unto you, Except ye eat the flesh of the Son of man and drink his blood, ye have not life in yourselves. He that eateth my flesh and drinketh my blood hath eternal life; and I will raise him up at the last day."

13. The bread from heaven the fathers ate in the wilderness, as Christ says here, was powerless to keep them from dying; but this bread makes immortal. If we believe on Christ, death cannot harm us; yea, it is no longer death. The Lord utters the same truth in another passage when he says to the Jews: "Verily, verily, I say unto you, If a man keep my Word, he shall never see death" (John 8:51). Here he speaks definitely of the Word of faith, and of the Gospel.

14. But one may say, as did the Jews, who took offense at these words of the Lord: The saints, nevertheless, died, and Abraham and the prophets likewise died. We reply to this: The death of Christians is only a sleep, as the Scriptures everywhere call it. A Christian neither tastes nor sees death; that is, he is never conscious of any death; for this Saviour, Christ Jesus, in whom he believes, has destroyed death so that he no longer needs to taste it and pay its penalty. Death is to the Christians only a transition of life, yea, a door to life: as Christ says in John 5:24: "Verily, verily, I say unto you, He that heareth my Word, and believeth him that sent me, hath eternal life., and cometh not into judgment, but hath passed out of death into life."

15. Therefore, a Christian life is a life of bliss and joy. Christ's yoke is easy

and sweet; the reason it seems to us galling and heavy is that the Father has not yet drawn us. and so we have no pleasure in it, neither does this Gospel lesson minister comfort to us. If we, however, rightly appropriated the words of Christ, they would be of much greater comfort to us. By faith we partake of this bread that has come down from heaven, Christ the Lord, when we believe on him as our Saviour and Redeemer.

16. In this light I now remind you that these words are not to be misconstrued and made to refer to the Sacrament of the Altar; whoever so interprets them does violence to this Gospel text. There is not a letter in it that refers to the Lord's Supper. Why should Christ here have in mind that Sacrament when it was not yet instituted? The whole chapter from which this Gospel is taken speaks of nothing but the spiritual food, namely, faith. When the people followed the Lord merely hoping again to eat and drink, as the Lord himself charges them with doing, he took the figure from the temporal food they sought, and speaks throughout the entire chapter of a spiritual food. He says: "The words that I have spoken unto you are spirit, and are life." Thereby he shows that he feeds them with the object of inducing them to believe on him, and that as they partook of the temporal food, so should they also partake of the spiritual. On this subject we will say more at some other time.

17. Now let us here notice that the Lord approaches us so lovingly and graciously, and offers us himself--his flesh and blood--in such gentle words that it should in all reason move the heart to believe on him; to believe that this bread, his flesh and blood, born of the Virgin Mary, was given because he had to pay the penalty of death and suffer in our stead the torments of hell, and, besides, to suffer the guilt of sins he never committed, as if they were his own. This he did willingly and received us as brethren and sisters. If we believe this we do the will of the heavenly Father, which is nothing else than that we believe on the Son. Christ says, just before our text: "This is the will of my Father, that every one that beholdeth the Son, and believeth on him, should have eternal life; and I will raise him up at the last day" (I John 6:40).

18. It is now evident that whoever has faith in this bread of heaven--in Christ, in this flesh and blood, of which he here speaks that it is given to him and that it is his--he also accepts it as his own, and has already done the will of God and eaten of this heavenly manna; as Augustine says: What do you prepare for your mouth? Only believe, and you have already eaten.

19. The whole New Testament treats of this spiritual supper, and especially does John here. The Sacrament of the Altar is a testament and confirmation of this true supper, with which we should strengthen our faith and be assured that this body and this blood, which we receive in the Sacrament has rescued us from sin and death, the devil, hell and all misery. Concerning this I have spoken and written more on other occasions.

20. What is the proof by which one may know that this heavenly bread is his and that he is invited to such a spiritual supper? He needs only to look at his

own heart. If he finds it so disposed that it is softened and cheered by God's promises and is firm in the conviction that it may appropriate this
bread of life, then he may be assured that he is one of the invited; for as one believes, even so is it done unto him. >From that moment on, he loves his neighbor and helps him as his brother; he rescues him, gives to him, loans to him and does nothing for him but that which he would desire his neighbor to do for himself. All this is attributable to the fact that Christ's kindness to him has leavened his heart with sweetness and love, so that he has pleasure and joy in serving his neighbor; yea, he is even in misery if he has no one to whom to show kindness. Besides all this, he is gently and humbly disposed toward everybody; he does not highly esteem the transient pomps of the world; he accepts everyone as he is, speaks evil of no one, interprets all things for the best where he sees things are not going right. When his neighbors are lacking in faith, in love, in life, then he prays for them, and he is heartily sorry when anyone gives offense to God or to his neighbor. To sum up all, with him the root and sap are good, for he is grafted into a rich and fruitful vine, in Christ; therefore, such fruits must come forth.

21. But if one has not faith and is not taught of God--if he never eats of this bread from heaven--he surely never brings forth these fruits. For where such fruits are not produced, there is certainly no true faith. St. Peter teaches us in 2 Peter 1:10 that we should make our calling unto salvation sure by good works; there he is really speaking of the works of love, of serving one's neighbor and treating him as one's own flesh and blood. This is sufficient on this Gospel. Let us pray for God's grace.

Of The Office of Preaching

Of the Office of Preaching & of Preachers and Hearers:

JOHN 10: 1-11: Verily, verily, I say unto you, He that entereth not by the door into the sheepfold, but climbeth up some other way, the same is a thief and a robber. But he that entereth in by the door is the shepherd of the sheep. To him the porter openeth; and the sheep hear his voice: and he calleth his own sheep by name, and leadeth them out. And when he putteth forth his own sheep, he goeth before them, and the sheep follow him: for they know his voice. And a stranger will they not follow, but will flee from him: for they know not the voice of strangers. This parable spake Jesus unto them: but they understood not what things they were which he spake unto them. Then said Jesus unto them again, Verily, verily, I say unto you, I am the door of the sheep. All that ever came before me are thieves and robbers: but the sheep did not hear them. I am the door: by me if any man enter in, he shall be saved, and shall go in and out, and find pasture. The thief cometh not, but for to steal, and to kill, and to destroy: I am come that they might have life, and that they might have it more abundantly. I am the good shepherd: the good shepherd giveth his life for the sheep.

Section I. True Preachers of the Word must Be Regularly Called.

1. This Gospel treats of the office of the ministry, how it is constituted, what it accomplishes and how it is misused. It is indeed very necessary to know these things, for the office of preaching is second to none in Christendom. St. Paul highly esteemed this office for the reason that through it the Word of God was proclaimed which is effective to the salvation of all who believe it. He says to the Romans (1:16): "I am not ashamed of the Gospel, for it is the power of God unto salvation to every one that believeth." We must now consider this theme, since our Gospel lesson presents and includes it. It will, however, be a stench in the nostrils of the pope! But how shall I deal differently with him? The text says: "He that entereth not by the door into the fold of the sheep, but climbeth up some other way, the same is a thief and a robber (murderer)."

2. This verse has been explained as having reference to those who climb, by their presumption, into the best church livings through favor and wealth, recommendations or their own power, not obtaining them by regular appointment and authority. And at present the most pious jurists are punishing people for running to Rome after fees and benefices, or after ecclesiastical preferment and offices. This they call simony. The practice is truly deplorable, for much depends upon being regularly called and appointed. No one should step into the office and preach from his own presumption and without a commission from those having the authority. But under present conditions, if we should wait until we received a commission to preach and to administer the sacraments, we would never perform those offices as long as we live. For the bishops in our day press into their offices by force, and those who have the power of preferment are influenced by friendship and rank. But I pass this by, and will speak of the true office, into which no one forces his way (even though his devotion urge him) without being called by others having the authority.

3. True, we all have authority to preach, yea, we must preach God's name; we are commanded to do so. Peter says in his first Epistle, (2:9-10) "But ye are an elect race, a royal priesthood, a holy nation, a people for God's own possession, that ye may show forth the excellencies of him who called you out of darkness into his marvellous light: who in time past were no people, but now are the people of God: who had not obtained mercy, but now have obtained mercy." Nevertheless, Paul establishes order in 1 Cor. 14:40 and says: "In whatever you do among yourselves, let everything be done decently and in order." In a family there must be order. If all the heirs strive for lordship, anarchy will reign in the family. If, however, by common consent, one of the number is selected for the heirship, the others withdrawing, harmony will obtain. Likewise, in the matter of preaching we must make selection that order may be preserved...

Section II. Preachers of the Word to Preach Nothing but the Word.

4. So much for the call into the office. But Christ is not speaking of that here; for something more is required, namely, that no rival or supplementary doctrine be introduced, nor another word be taught than Christ has taught. Christ says in Mt. 23:2-4: "The scribes and the Pharisees sit on Moses' seat: all things therefore whatsoever they bid you, these do and observe: but do not ye after their works; for they say and do not. Yea, they bind heavy burdens too grievous to be borne, and lay them on men's shoulders; but they themselves will not move them with their finger." Although these of whom Christ here speaks were regularly appointed, yet they were thieves and murderers; for they taught variations from Christ's teaching. Christ reproves them in another place, in Matthew 15:3, where he holds up before them their traditions and tells them how, through their own inventions, they have transgressed the commandments

of God, yea, totally abolished them. We have also many prophets who were regularly appointed and still were misled, like Balaam, of whom we read in Num. 22; also Nathan, described in 2 Sam 7:3. Similarly many bishops have erred.

5. Here Christ says: He who would enter by the door must be ready to speak the Word concerning Christ and his word must center in Christ. Let it be called "coming" when one preaches aright; the approaching is spiritual, and through the Word--upon the ears of his hearers, the preacher comes at last into the sheepfold--the heart of believers. Christ says that the shepherd must enter by the door; that is, preach nothing but Christ, for Christ is the door into the sheepfold.

6. But where there are intruders, who make their own door, their own hole to crawl through, their own addition different from that which Christ taught, they are thieves. Of these Paul says to the Romans (16:17-18): "Now I beseech you, brethren, mark them that are causing the divisions and occasions of stumbling, contrary to the doctrine which ye learned: and turn away from them. For they that are such serve not our Lord Christ, but their own belly; and by their smooth and fair speech they beguile the hearts of the innocent." Paul does not speak of opposing or antagonistic doctrines, but of those placed beside the true doctrine; they are additions, making divisions. Paul calls it a rival doctrine, an addition, an occasion of stumbling, an offense and a byway, when one establishes the conscience upon his own goodness or deeds.

7. Now, the Gospel is sensitive, complete and pre-eminent: it must be intolerant of additions and rival teachings. The doctrine of earning entrance into heaven by virtue of fastings, prayers and penance is a branch road, which the Gospel will not tolerate. But our Church authorities endorse these things, hence they are thieves and murderers; for they do violence to our consciences, which is slaying and destroying the sheep. How is this accomplished? If only I am directed into a branch or parallel road, then my soul is turned from God upon that road, where I must perish. Thus this road is the cause of my death. The conscience and heart of man must be founded upon one single Word or they will come to grief. "All flesh is grass, and all the goodliness thereof is as the flower of the field" (Is 40:6).

8. The doctrines of men, however admirable, fall to the ground, and with them the conscience that has built upon them. There is no help nor remedy. But the Word of God is eternal and must endure forever; no devil can overthrow it. The foundation is laid upon which the conscience may be established forever. The words of men must perish and everything that cleaves to them. Those who enter not by the door--that is, those who do not speak the true and pure Word of God, without any addition--do not lay the right foundation; they destroy and torture and slaughter the sheep. Therefore, Christ says further in this Gospel: "But he that entereth in by the door is the shepherd of the sheep. To him the porter openeth; and the sheep hear his Voice."

Section III. A True Preacher Should First Use the Law Aright and Then Preach the Gospel.

9. The porter here is the preacher who rightly teaches the Law--shows that the Law exists and must reveal to us our helplessness; that the works of the Law do not help us, and yet they are insistent. He then opens to the shepherd, that is, to Christ the Lord, and lets him alone feed the sheep. For the office of the Law is at an end; it has accomplished its mission of revealing to the heart its sins until it is completely humbled. Then Christ comes and makes a lamb out of the sheep--feeds it with his Gospel and directs it how to regain cheer for the heart so hopelessly troubled and crushed by the Law.

10. The lamb then hears Christ's voice and follows it. It has the choicest of pastures, and knows the voice of the shepherd. But the voice of a stranger it never hears and never follows. Just as soon as one preaches to it about works, it is worried and its heart cannot receive the teaching with joy. It knows very well that nothing is accomplished by means of works; for one may do as much as he will, still he carries a heavy spirit and he thinks he has not done enough, nor done rightly. But when the Gospel comes--the voice of the shepherd--it says: God gave to the world his only Son, that all who believe on him should not perish, but have everlasting life. Then is the heart happy; it feeds upon these words and finds them good. The lamb has found its satisfying pasture; it wants none other. Yea, when it is given other pasture, it flees from it and will not feed therein. This pasture always attracts the sheep, and the sheep also find it. God says in the prophecy of Isaiah: "So shall my Word be that goeth forth out of my mouth: it shall not return unto me void, but it shall accomplish all in the things whereto, I sent it" (Is 55:11).

Section IV. The Hearers Have the Right to Examine and Judge a Sermon

"And he calleth his own sheep by name, and leadeth them out. When he hath put forth all his own, he goeth before them and the sheep follow him; for they know his voice. And a stranger will they not follow, but will flee from him; for they know not the voice of strangers."

11. In this text there are two thoughts worthy of note: the liberty of faith, and the power to judge. You know that our soul-murderers have proposed to us that what the councils and the learned doctors decide and decree, that we should accept, and not judge for ourselves whether it is right or not. They have become so certain of the infallibility of the councils and doctors that they have now established the edict, publicly seen, that if we do not accept what they say, we are put under the ban. Now, let us take a spear in hand and make a hole in their shield; yea, their resolutions shall be a spider's web. And you should, moreover, use upon them the spear which until now they have used upon us,

and hold before them its point.

12. Remember well that the sheep have to pass judgment upon that which is placed before them. They should say: We have Christ as our Lord and prefer his Word to the words of any man or to those of the angels of darkness. We want to examine and judge for ourselves whether the pope, the bishops and their followers do right or not. For Christ says here that the sheep judge and know which is the right voice and which is not. Now let them come along. Have they decreed anything? We will examine whether it is right, and according to our own judgment interpret that which is a private affair for each individual Christian, knowing that the authority to do this is not human, but divine. Even the real sheep flee from a stranger and hold to the voice of their shepherd.

13. Upon this authority., the Gospel knocks all the councils, all the papistic laws, to the ground, granting to us that we should receive nothing without judging it, that we have besides the power to judge, and that such judgment stands until the present day. The papists have taken from us the sword, so that we have not been able to repel any false doctrine, and, moreover, they have by force introduced false teachings among us. If now we take the sword from them they will be sorry. And we must truly take it, not by force, but by means of the Word, letting go all else that we have, saying: I am God's sheep, whose Word I wish to appropriate to myself. If you will give me that, I will acknowledge you to be a shepherd. If you, however, add another Gospel to this one, and do not give me the pure Gospel, then I will not consider you a shepherd, and will not listen to your voice; for the office of which you boast extends no farther than the Word goes. If we find one to be a shepherd, we should receive him as such: if he is not, we should remove him; for the sheep shall judge the voice of the shepherd. If he does not give us the right kind of pasture, we should bid farewell to such a shepherd, that is, to the bishop; for a hat of pearls and a staff of silver do not make a shepherd or a bishop, but rather does the office depend upon his care of the sheep and their pasture.

14. Now the papists object to judgment being passed upon any of their works; for this reason they have intruded and taken from us the sword which we might use for such a purpose. Also, they dictate that we must accept, without any right of judgment, whatever they propose. And it has almost come to such a pass that whenever the pope breathes they make an article of faith out of it, and they have proclaimed that the authorities have the right to pass such laws for their subjects as they desire, independent of the judgment of the latter. These conditions mean ruin to the Christians, so much so that a hundred thousand swords should be desired for one pope. This they know very well, and they cling hard to their laws. If they would permit unbiased judgment, their laws would be set aside and they would have to preach the pure Word; but such a course would reduce the size of their stomachs and the number of their horses.

15. Therefore, be ye aroused by this passage of Scripture to hew to pieces

and thrust through everything that is not in harmony with the Gospel, for it belongs to the sheep to judge, and not to the preachers. You have the authority and power to judge everything that is preached; that and nothing less. If we have not this power, then Christ vainly said to us in Mt. 7:15: "Beware of false prophets, who come to you in sheep's clothing, but inwardly are ravening wolves." We could not beware if we had not the power to judge, but were obliged to accept everything they said and preached.

V. Preachers Are to Force No One to Believe.

16. The second thought is, no one shall be forced to believe; for the sheep follow him whom they know and flee from strangers. Now, Christ's wish is that none be forced, but that they be permitted to follow from willing hearts and of their own desire; not out of fear, shame or strife. He would let the Word go forth and accomplish all. When their hearts are taken captive, then they will surely come of themselves. Faith does not go forth from the heart unless it has the Word of God.

17. Our noblemen are now mad and foolish in that they undertake to drive people to believe by means of force and the sword. Christ here wishes the sheep to come of themselves, from their knowledge of his voice. The body may be forced, as the pope, for example, has by his laws coerced people to go to confession and to the Lord's Supper, but the heart cannot be taken captive. Christ wants it to be free. Although he had power to coerce men, he wished to win them through his pleasing, loving preaching. Whoever lays hold of Christ's word follows after him and permits nothing to, tear him from it. The noblemen wish to drive the people to believe by means of the sword and fire; that is nonsense. Then let us see to it that we allow the pure Word of God to take its course, and afterward leave them free to follow, whom it has taken captive; yea, they will follow voluntarily.

18. By this I do not wish to abolish the civil sword; for the hand can hold it within its grasp so that it does no one any harm, but it holds it inactive. It must be retained because of wicked villains who have no regard at all for the Word; but the sword cannot force the heart and bring it to faith. In view of its inability, it must keep silent in matters of faith; here one must enter by the door, and preach the Word and make the heart free. Only in this way are men led to believe. These are the two expedients--for the pious and the wicked: the pious are to be drawn by the Word, and the wicked to be driven by the sword to observe order.

VI. The Marks of False Preachers.

19. Now, Christ interprets his own words. He says that he is the door to the sheep, but all the others who came before him, that is, those who were not sent by God as the prophets were, but came of themselves, uncommissioned, are thieves and murderers; they steal his honor from God and strangle human souls

by their false doctrines. But Christ is the door, and whoever enters by him will be saved, and will go in and out and find pasture. Here Christ speaks of the Christian liberty, which means that Christians are now free from the curse and the tyranny of the Law, and may keep the Law or not, according as they see that the love and need of their neighbor requires. This is what Paul did. When he was among the Jews, he kept the Law with the Jews; when among the gentiles, he kept it as they kept it, which he himself says in 1 Cor. 9:19-23:

"For though I was free from all men, I brought myself under bondage to all, that I might gain the more. And to the Jews I became as a Jew, that I might gain Jews; to them that are under the law, as under the law, not being myself under the law, that I might gain them that are under the law; to them that are without law, as without law, not being without law to God, but under law to Christ, that I might gain them that are without law. To the weak I became weak, that I might gain the weak: I am become all things to all men, that I may by all means save some. And I do all things for the gospel's sake, that I may be a joint partaker thereof."

20. That, the thieves and murderers, the false teachers and prophets, never do; they accomplish nothing but to steal, strangle and destroy the sheep. But Christ, the true and faithful shepherd, comes only that the sheep may have life and be fully satisfied. This is enough on today's Gospel for the present. We will conclude and pray God for grace rightly to lay hold of it and understand it.

The Twofold Use of the Law & Gospel: "Letter" & "Spirit"

Second Corinthians 3:4-11. 4 And such confidence have we through Christ to Godward: 5 not that we are sufficient of ourselves, to account anything as from ourselves; but our sufficiency is from God; 6 who also made us sufficient as ministers of a new covenant; not of the letter, but of the spirit: for the letter killeth, but the spirit giveth life. 7 But if the ministration of death, written, and engraven on stones, came with glory, so that the children of Israel could not look stedfastly upon the face of Moses for the glory of his face; which glory was passing away: 8 how shall not rather the ministration of the spirit be with glory? 9 For if the ministration of condemnation hath glory, much rather doth the ministration of righteousness exceed in glory. 10 For verily that which hath been made glorious hath not been made glorious in this respect, by reason of the glory that surpasseth. 11 For if that which passeth away was with glory, much more that which remaineth is in glory.

Gospel Transcends Law

1. This epistle lesson sounds altogether strange and wonderful to individuals unaccustomed to Scripture language, particularly to that of Paul. To the inexperienced ear and heart it is not intelligible. In popedom thus far it has remained quite unapprehended, although reading of the words has been practiced.

2. That we may understand it, we must first get an idea of Paul's theme. Briefly, he would oppose the vain boasting of false apostles and preachers concerning their possession of the spirit and their peculiar skill and gifts, by praising and glorifying the office of a preacher of the Gospel with which he is intrusted. For he found that, especially in the Church at Corinth, which he had converted by the words of his own lips and brought to faith in Christ, soon after his departure the devil introduced his heresies whereby the people were turned from the truth and betrayed into other ways. Since it became his duty to make an attack upon such heresies, he devoted both his epistles to the purpose of keeping the Corinthians in the right way, so that they might retain the pure doctrine received from him, and beware of false spirits. The main thing which moved him to write this second epistle was his desire to emphasize to them his

apostolic office of a preacher of the Gospel, in order to put to shame the glory of those other teachers--the glory they boasted with many words and great pretense.

3. He starts in on this theme just before he reaches our text. And this is how it is he comes to speak in high terms of praise of the ministration of the Gospel and to contrast and compare the twofold ministration or message which may be proclaimed in the Church, provided, of course, that God's Word is to be preached and not the nonsense of human falsehood and the doctrine of the devil. One is that of the Old Testament, the other of the New; in other words, the office of Moses, or the Law, and the office of the Gospel of Christ. He contrasts the glory and power of the latter with those of the former, which, it is true, is also the Word of God. In this manner he endeavors to defeat the teachings and pretensions of those seductive spirits who, as he but lately foretold, pervert God"s Word, in that they greatly extol the Law of God, yet at best do not teach its right use, but, instead of making it tributary to faith in Christ, misuse it to teach work-righteousness.

4. Since the words before us are in reality a continuation of those with which the chapter opens, the latter must be considered in this connection. We read:

"Are we beginning again to commend ourselves? or need we, as do some, epistles of commendation to you or from you? Ye are our epistle, written in our hearts, known and read of all men; being made manifest that ye are an epistle of Christ, ministered by us, written not with ink, but with the Spirit of the living God; not in tables of stone, but in tables that are hearts of flesh."

"We, my fellow-apostles and co-laborers and I," he says, "do not ask for letters and seals from others commending us to you, or from you commending us to others, in order to seduce people after gaining their good will in your church and in others as well. Such is the practice of the false apostles, and many even now present letters and certificates from honest preachers and Churches, and make them the means whereby their unrighteous plotting may be received in good faith. Such letters, thank God, we stand not in need of, and you need not fear we shall use such means of deception. For you are yourselves the letter we have written and wherein we may pride ourselves and which we present everywhere. For it is a matter of common knowledge that you have been taught by us, and brought to Christ through our ministry."

Paul's Converts Living Epistles

5. Inasmuch as his activity among them is his testimonial, and they themselves are aware that through his ministerial office he has constituted them a church, he calls them an epistle written by himself; not with ink and in paragraphs, not on paper or wood, nor engraved upon hard rock as the Ten Commandments written upon tables of stone, which Moses placed before the people, but written by the Holy Spirit upon fleshly tables--hearts of tender flesh. The Spirit is the ink or the inscription, yes, even the writer himself; but the

pencil or pen and the hand of the writer is the ministry of Paul.

6. This figure of a written epistle is, however, in accord with Scripture usage. Moses commands (Deut 6:6-9; 11, 18) that the Israelites write the Ten Commandments in all places where they walked or stood upon the posts of their houses, and upon their gates, and ever have them before their eyes and in their hearts. Again (Prov 7:2-3), Solomon says: "Keep my commandments and...my law as the apple of thine eye. Bind them upon thy fingers; write them upon the tablet of thy heart." He speaks as a father to his child when giving the child an earnest charge to remember a certain thing--"Dear child, remember this; forget it not; keep it in thy heart." Likewise, God says in the book of Jeremiah the prophet (ch. 31, 33), "I will put my law in their inward parts, and in their heart will I write it." Here man's heart is represented as a sheet, or slate, or page, whereon is written the preached Word; for the heart is to receive and securely keep the Word. In this sense Paul says: "We have, by our ministry, written a booklet or letter upon your heart, which witnesses that you believe in God the Father, Son and Holy Ghost and have the assurance that through Christ you are redeemed and saved. This testimony is what is written on your heart. The letters are not characters traced with ink or crayon, but the living thoughts, the fire and force of the heart.

7. Note further, that it is his ministry to which Paul ascribes the preparation of their heart thereon and the inscription which constitutes them "living epistles of Christ." He contrasts his ministry with the blind fancies of those fanatics who seek to receive, and dream of having, the Holy Spirit without the oral word; who, perchance, creep into a corner and grasp the Spirit through dreams, directing the people away from the preached Word and visible ministry. But Paul says that the Spirit, through his preaching, has wrought in the hearts of his Corinthians, to the end that Christ lives and is mighty in them. After such statement he bursts into praise of the ministerial office, comparing the message, or preaching, of Moses with that of himself and the apostles. He says:

"Such confidence have we through Christ to Godward: not that we are sufficient of ourselves, to account anything as from ourselves; but our sufficiency is from God

True Preachers Commissioned by God

8. These words are blows and thrusts for the false apostles and preachers. Paul is mortal enemy to the blockheads who make great boast, pretending to what they do not possess and to what they cannot do; who boast of having the Spirit in great measure; who are ready to counsel and aid the whole world; who pride themselves on the ability to invent something new. It is to be a surpassingly precious and heavenly thing they are to spin out of their heads, as the dreams of pope and monks have been in time past.

"We do not so," says Paul. "We rely not upon ourselves or our wisdom and ability. We preach not what we have ourselves invented. But this is our boast and trust in Christ before God, that we have made of you a divine epistle; have written upon your hearts, not our thoughts, but the Word of God. We are not, however, glorifying our own power, but the works and the power of him who has called and equipped us for such an office; from whom proceeds all you have heard and believed.

9. It is a glory which every preacher may claim, to be able to say with full confidence of heart: "This trust have I toward God in Christ, that what I teach and preach is truly the Word of God." Likewise, when he performs other official duties in the Church--baptizes a child, absolves and comforts a sinner--it must be done in the same firm conviction that such is the command of Christ.

10. He who would teach and exercise authority in the Church without this glory, "it is profitable for him," as Christ says (Mt. 18:6), "that a great millstone should be hanged about his neck, and that he should be sunk in the depths of the sea." For the devil's lies he preaches, and death is what he effects. Our Papists, in time past, after much and long-continued teaching, after many inventions and works whereby they hoped to be saved, nevertheless always doubted in heart and mind whether or no they had pleased God. The teaching and works of all heretics and seditious spirits certainly do not bespeak for them trust in Christ; their own glory is the object of their teaching, and the homage and praise of the people is the goal of their desire. "Not that we are sufficient of ourselves, to account anything as from ourselves."

11. As said before, this is spoken in denunciation of the false spirits who believe that by reason of eminent equipment of special creation and election, they are called to come to the rescue of the people, expecting wonders from whatever they say and do.

Human Doctrine No Place in the Church

12. Now, we know ourselves to be of the same clay whereof they are made; indeed, we perhaps have the greater call from God: yet we cannot boast of being capable of ourselves to advise or aid men. We cannot even originate an idea calculated to give help. And when it comes to the knowledge of how one may stand before God and attain to eternal life, that is truly not to be achieved by our work or power, nor to originate in our brain. In other things, those pertaining to this temporal life, you may glory in what You know, you may advance the teachings of reason, you may invent ideas of your own; for example: how to make shoes or clothes, how to govern a household, how to manage a herd. In such things exercise your mind to the best of your ability. Cloth or leather of this sort will permit itself to be stretched and cut according to the good pleasure of the tailor or shoemaker. But in spiritual matters, human reasoning certainly is not in order; other intelligence, other skill and power, are requisite here--something to be granted by God himself and revealed through his Word.

13. What mortal has ever discovered or fathomed the truth that the three

persons in the eternal divine essence are one God; that the second person, the Son of God, was obliged to become man, born of a virgin; and that no way of life could be opened for us, save through his crucifixion? Such truth never would have been heard nor preached, would never in all eternity have been published, learned and believed, had not God himself revealed it.

14. For this season they are blind fools of first magnitude and dangerous characters who would boast of their grand performances, and think that the people are served when they preach their own fancies and inventions. It has been the practice in the Church for anyone to introduce any teaching he saw fit; for example, the monks and priests have daily produced new saints, pilgrimages, special prayers, works and sacrifices in the effort to blot out sin, redeem souls from purgatory, and so on. They who make up things of this kind are not such as put their trust in God through Christ, but rather such as defy God and Christ. Into the hearts of men, where Christ alone should be, they shove the filth and write the lies of the devil. Yet they think themselves, and themselves only, qualified for all essential teaching and work, self-grown doctors that they are, saints all-powerful without the help of God and Christ.

"But our sufficiency is from God."

15. Of ourselves--in our own wisdom and strength--we cannot effect, discover nor teach any counsel or help for man, whether for ourselves or others. Any good work we perform among you, any doctrine we write upon your heart that is God's own work. He puts into our heart and mouth what we should say, and impresses it upon your heart through the Holy Spirit. Therefore, we cannot ascribe to ourselves any honor therein, cannot seek our own glory as the self-instructed and proud spirits do; we must give to God alone the honor, and must glory in the fact that by his grace and power he works in you unto Salvation, through the office committed unto us.

16. Now, Paul's thought here is that nothing should be taught and practiced in the Church but what is unquestionably God's Word. It will not do to introduce or perform anything whatever upon the strength of man's judgment. Man's achievements, man's reasoning and power, are of no avail save in so far as they come from God. As Peter says in his first epistle (ch. 4:11): "If any man speaketh, speaking as it were oracles of God; if any man ministereth, ministering as of the strength which God supplieth." In short, let him who would be wise, who would boast of great skill, talents and power, confine himself to things other than spiritual; with respect to spiritual matters, let him keep his place and refrain from boasting and pretense. For it is of no moment that men observe your greatness and ability; the important thing is that poor souls may rest assured of being presented with God's Word and works, whereby they may be saved.

"Who also made us sufficient as ministers of a new covenant; not of the letter, but of the spirit: for the letter killeth, but the spirit giveth life."

The New Covenant

17. Paul here proceeds to exalt the office and power of the Gospel over the glorying of the false apostles, and to elevate the power of the Word above that of all other doctrine, even of the Law of God. Truly we are not sufficient of ourselves and have nothing to boast of so far as human activity is considered. For that is without merit or power, however strenuous the effort may be to fulfil God's Law. We have, however, something infinitely better to boast of, something not grounded in our own activity: by God we have been made sufficient for a noble ministry, termed the ministry "of a New Covenant." This ministry is not only exalted far above any teaching to be evolved by human wisdom, skill and power, but is more glorious than the ministry termed the "Old Covenant," which in time past was delivered to the Jews through Moses. While this ministry clings, in common with other doctrine, to the Word given by revelation, it is the agency whereby the Holy Spirit works in the heart. Therefore, Paul says it is not a ministration of the letter, but "of the spirit."

"Spirit" & "Letter"

18. This passage relative to spirit and letter has in the past been wholly strange language to us. Indeed, to such extent has man's nonsensical interpretation perverted and weakened it that I, through a learned doctor of the holy Scriptures, failed to understand it altogether, and I could find no one to teach me. And to this day it is unintelligible to all popedom. In fact, even the old teachers--Origen, Jerome and others--have not caught Paul's thought. And no wonder, truly! For it is essentially a doctrine far beyond the power of man's intelligence to comprehend. When human reason meddles with it, it becomes perplexed. The doctrine is wholly unintelligible to it, for human thought goes no farther than the Law and the Ten Commandments. Laying hold upon these it confines itself to them. It does not attempt to do more, being governed by the principle that unto him who fulfils the demands of the Law, or commandments, God is gracious. Reason knows nothing about the wretchedness of depraved nature. It does not recognize the fact that no man is able to keep God's commandments; that all are under sin and condemnation; and that the only way whereby help could be received was for God to give his Son for the world, ordaining another ministration, one through which grace and reconciliation might be proclaimed to us. Now, he who does not understand the sublime subject of which Paul speaks cannot but miss the true meaning of his words. How much more did we invite this fate when we threw the Scriptures and Saint Paul's epistles under the bench, and, like swine in husks, wallowed in man's nonsense! Therefore, we must submit to correction and learn to understand the apostle's utterance aright.

19. "Letter" and "spirit" have been understood to mean, according to Origen and Jerome, the obvious sense of the written word. St. Augustine, it must be admitted, has gotten an inkling of the truth. Now, the position of the former

teachers would perhaps not be quite incorrect did they correctly explain the words. By "literary sense" they signify the meaning of a Scripture narrative according to the ordinary interpretation of the words. By "spiritual sense" they signify the secondary, hidden sense found in the words.

For instance: The Scripture narrative in Genesis third records how the serpent persuaded the woman to eat of the forbidden fruit and to give to her husband, who also ate. This narrative in its simplest meaning represents what they understand by "letter." "Spirit," however, they understand to mean the spiritual interpretation, which is thus: The serpent signifies the evil temptation which lures to sin. The woman represents the sensual state, or the sphere in which such enticements and temptations make themselves felt. Adam, the man, stands for reason, which is called man's highest endowment. Now, when reason does not yield to the allurements of external sense, all is well; but when it permits itself to waver and consent, the fall has taken place.

20. Origen was the first to trifle thus with the holy Scriptures, and many others followed, until now it is thought to be the sign of great cleverness for the Church to be filled with such quibblings. The aim is to imitate Paul, who (Gal 4;22-24) figuratively interprets the story of Abraham's two sons, the one by the free woman, or the mistress of the house, and the other by the hand-maid. The two women, Paul says, represent the two covenants: one covenant makes only bondservants, which is just what he in our text terms the ministration of the letter; the other leads to liberty, or, as he says here, the ministration of the spirit, which gives life. And the two sons are the two peoples, one of which does not go farther than the Law, while the other accepts in faith the Gospel.

True, this is an interpretation not directly suggested by the narrative and the text. Paul himself calls it an allegory; that is, a mystic narrative, or a story with a hidden meaning. But he does not say that the literal text is necessarily the letter that killeth, and the allegory, or hidden meaning, the spirit. But the false teachers assert of all Scripture that the text, or record itself, is but a dead "letter," its interpretation being "the spirit." Yet they have not pushed interpretation farther than the teaching of the Law; and it is precisely the Law which Paul means when he speaks of "the letter."

21. Paul employs the word "letter" in such contemptuous sense in reference to the Law--though the Law is, nevertheless, the Word of God--when he compares it with the ministry of the Gospel. The letter is to him the doctrine of the Ten Commandments, which teach how we should obey God, honor parents, love our neighbor, and so on--the very best doctrine to be found in all books, sermons and schools.

The word "letter" is to the apostle Paul everything which may take the form of doctrine, of literary arrangement, of record, so long as it remains something spoken or written. Also thoughts which may be pictured or expressed by word or writing, but it is not that which is written in the heart, to become its life. "Letter" is the whole Law of Moses, or the Ten Commandments, though the supreme authority of such teaching is not denied. It matters not whether you hear them, read them, or reproduce them mentally. For instance, when I sit down to meditate upon the first commandment: "Thou shalt have no other gods before me," or the second, or the third, and so forth, I have something which I can read, write, discuss, and aim to fulfil with all my might. The process is quite similar when the emperor or prince gives a command and says: "This you shall do, that you shall eschew." This is what the apostle calls "the letter," or, as we have called it on another occasion, the written sense.

22. Now, as opposed to "the letter," there is another doctrine or message, which he terms the "ministration of a New Covenant" and "of the Spirit." This doctrine does not teach what works are required of man, for that man has already heard; but it makes known to him what God would do for him and bestow upon him, indeed what he has already done: he has given his Son Christ for us; because, for our disobedience to the Law, which no man fulfils, we were under God's wrath and condemnation. Christ made satisfaction for our sins, effected a reconciliation with God and gave to us his own righteousness. Nothing is said in this ministration of man's deeds; it tells rather of the works of Christ, who is unique in that he was born of a virgin, died for sin and rose from the dead, something no other man has been able to do. This doctrine is revealed through none but the Holy Spirit, and none other confers the Holy Spirit. The Holy Spirit works in the hearts of them who hear and accept the doctrine. Therefore, this ministration is termed a ministration "of the Spirit."

23. The apostle employs the words "letter" and "spirit," to contrast the two doctrines; to emphasize his office and show its advantage over all others, however eminent the teachers whom they boast, and however great the spiritual unction which they vaunt. It is of design that he does not term the two dispensations "Law" and "Gospel," but names them according to the respective effects produced. He honors the Gospel with a superior term--"ministration of the spirit." Of the Law, on the contrary, he speaks almost contemptuously, as if he would not honor it with the title of God's commandment, which in reality it is, according to his own admission later on that its deliverance to Moses and its injunction upon the children of Israel was an occasion of surpassing glory.

24. Why does Paul choose this method? Is it right for one to despise or dishonor God's Law? Is not a chaste and honorable life a matter of beauty and godliness? Such facts, it may be contended, are implanted by God in reason itself, and all books teach them; they are the governing force in the world. I reply: Paul's chief concern is to defeat the vainglory and pretensions of false preachers, and to teach them the right conception and appreciation of the Gospel which he proclaimed. What Paul means is this: When the Jews vaunt their Law of Moses, which was received as Law from God and recorded upon two tables of stone; when they vaunt their learned and saintly preachers of the Law and its exponents, and hold their deeds and manner of life up to admiration, what is all that compared to the Gospel message? The claim may

be well made: a fine sermon, a splendid exposition; but, after all, nothing more comes of it than precepts, expositions, written comments. The precept, "Thou shalt love the Lord thy God with all thy heart, and thy neighbor as thyself," remains a mere array of words. When much time and effort have been spent in conforming one's life to it, nothing has been accomplished. You have pods without peas, husks without kernels.

25. For it is impossible to keep the Law without Christ, though man may, for the sake of honor or property, or from fear of punishment, feign outward holiness. The heart which does not discern God's grace in Christ cannot turn to God nor trust in him; it cannot love his commandments and delight in them, but rather resists them. For nature rebels at compulsion. No man likes to be a captive in chains. One does not voluntarily bow to the rod of punishment or submit to the executioner's sword; rather, because of these things, his anger against the Law is but increased, and he ever thinks: "Would that I might unhindered steal, rob, hoard, gratify my lust, and so on!" And when restrained by force, he would there were no Law and no God. And this is the case where conduct shows some effects of discipline, in that the outer man has been subjected to the teaching of the Law.

26. But in a far more appalling degree does inward rebellion ensue when the heart feels the full force of the Law; when, standing before God's judgment, it feels the sentence of condemnation; as we shall presently hear, for the apostle says "the letter killeth." Then the truly hard knots appear. Human nature fumes and rages against the Law; offenses appear in the heart, the fruit of hate and enmity against the Law; and presently human nature flees before God and is incensed at God's judgment. It begins to question the equity of his dealings, to ask if he is a just God. Influenced by such thoughts, it falls ever deeper into doubt, it murmurs and chafes, until finally, unless the Gospel comes to the rescue, it utterly despairs, as did Judas, and Saul, and perhaps pass out of this life with God and creation. This is what Paul means when he says (Rom 7:8-9) that the Law works sin in the heart of man, and sin works death, or kills.

27. You see, then, why the Law is called "the letter": though noble doctrine, it remains on the surface; it does not enter the heart as a vital force which begets obedience. Such is the baseness of human nature, it will not and cannot conform to the Law; and so corrupt is mankind, there is no individual who does not violate all God's commandments in spite of daily hearing the preached Word and having held up to view God's wrath and eternal condemnation. Indeed, the harder pressed man is, the more furiously he storms against the Law.

28. The substance of the matter is this: When all the commandments have been put together, when their message receives every particle of praise to which it is entitled, it is still a mere letter. That is, teaching not put into practice. By "letter" is signified all manner of law, doctrine and message, which goes no farther than the oral or written word, which consists only of the powerless letter. To illustrate: A law promulgated by a prince or the authorities of a city,

if not enforced, remains merely an open letter, which makes a demand indeed, but ineffectually. Similarly, God's Law, although a teaching of supreme authority and the eternal will of God, must suffer itself to become a mere empty letter or husk. Without a quickening heart, and devoid of fruit, the Law is powerless to effect life and salvation. It may well be called a veritable table of omissions (Lass-tafel); that is, it is a written enumeration, not of duties performed but of duties cast aside. In the languages of the world, it is a royal edict which remains unobserved and unperformed. In this light St. Augustine understood the Law. He says, commenting on Psalm 17, "What is Law without grace but a letter without spirit?" Human nature, without the aid of Christ and his grace, cannot keep it.

29. Again, Paul in terming the Gospel a "ministration of the spirit" would call attention to its power to produce in the hearts of men an effect wholly different from that of the Law: it is accompanied by the Holy Spirit and it creates a new heart. Man, driven into fear and anxiety by the preaching of the Law, hears this Gospel message, which, instead of reminding him of God's demands, tells him what God has done for him. It points not to man's works, but to the works of Christ, and bids him confidently believe that for the sake of his Son God will forgive his sins and accept him as his child. And this message, when received in faith, immediately cheers and comforts the heart. The heart will no longer flee from God; rather it turns to him. Finding grace with God and experiencing his mercy, the heart feels drawn to him. It commences to call upon him and to treat and revere him as its beloved God. In proportion as such faith and solace grow, also love for the commandments will grow and obedience to them will be man's delight. Therefore, God would have his Gospel message urged unceasingly as the means of awakening man's heart to discern his state and recall the great grace and lovingkindness of God, with the result that the power of the Holy Spirit is increased constantly. Note, no influence of the Law, no work of man is present here. The force is a new and heavenly one--the power of the Holy Spirit. He impresses upon the heart Christ and his works, making of it a true book which does not consist in the tracery of mere letters and words, but in true life and action.

30. God promised of old, in Joel 2:28 and other passages, to give the Spirit through the new message, the Gospel. And he has verified his promise by public manifestations in connection with the preaching of that Gospel, as on the day of Pentecost and again later. When the apostles, Peter and others, began to preach, the Holy Spirit descended visibly from heaven upon their hearts. Acts 8:17; 10:44. Up to that time, throughout the period the Law was preached, no one had heard or seen such manifestation. The fact could not but be grasped that this was a vastly different message from that of the Law when such mighty results followed in its train. And yet its substance was no more than what Paul declared (Acts 13:38-39): "Through this man is proclaimed unto you remission

of sins: and by him every one that believeth is justified from all things, from which ye could not be justified by the law of Moses."

31. In this teaching you see no more the empty letters, the valueless husks or shells of the Law, which unceasingly enjoins., "This thou shalt do and observe," and ever in vain. You see instead the true kernel and power which confers Christ and the fullness of His Spirit. In consequence, men heartily believe the message of the Gospel and enjoy its riches. They are accounted as having fulfilled the Ten Commandments. John says (Jn 1:16-17): "Of his fullness we all received, and grace for grace. For the Law was given through Moses; grace and truth came through Jesus Christ." John's thought is: The Law has indeed been given by Moses, but what avails that fact? To be sure, it is a noble doctrine and portrays a beautiful and instructive picture of man's duty to God and all mankind; it is really excellent as to the letter. Yet it remains empty; it does not enter into the heart. Therefore it is called "law," nor can it become aught else, so long as nothing more is given.

Christ Supersedes Moses

Before there can be fulfilment, another than Moses must come, bringing another doctrine. Instead of a law enjoined, there must be grace and truth revealed. For to enjoin a command and to embody the truth are two different things; just as teaching and doing differ. Moses, it is true, teaches the doctrine of the Law, so far as exposition is concerned, but he can neither fulfil it himself nor give others the ability to do so. That it might be fulfilled, God's Son had to come with his fullness; he has fulfilled the Law for himself and it is he who communicates to our empty heart the power to attain to the same fullness.

This becomes possible when we receive grace for grace, that is, when we come to the enjoyment of Christ, and for the sake of him who enjoys with God fullness of grace, although our own obedience to the Law is still imperfect. Being possessed of solace and grace, we receive by his power the Holy Spirit also, so that, instead of harboring mere empty letters within us, we come to the truth and begin to fulfil God's Law, in such a way, however, that we draw from his fullness and drink from that as a fountain.

Christ the Source of Life Greater than Adam the Source of Death

32. Paul gives us the same thought in Romans 5:17-18, where he compares Adam and Christ. Adam, he says, by his disobedience in Paradise, became the source of sin and death in the world; by the sin of this one man, condemnation passed upon all men. But on the other hand, Christ, by his obedience and righteousness, has become for us the abundant source wherefrom all may obtain righteousness and the power of obedience. And with respect to the latter source, it is far richer and more abundant than the former. While by the single

sin of one man, sin and death passed upon all men, to wax still more powerful with the advent of the Law, of such surpassing strength and greatness, on the other hand, is the grace and bounty which we have in Christ that it not only washes away the particular sin of the one man Adam, which, until Christ came, overwhelmed all men in death, but overwhelms and blots out all sin whatever. Thus they who receive his fullness of grace and bounty unto righteousness are, according to Paul, lords of life through Jesus Christ alone.

The Law Ineffectual

33. You see now how the two messages differ, and why Paul exalts the one, the preaching of the Gospel, and calls it a "ministration of the spirit," but terms the other, the Law, a mere empty "letter." His object is to humble the pride of the false apostles and preachers which they felt in their Judaism and the law of Moses, telling the people with bold pretensions: "Beloved, let Paul preach what he will, he cannot overthrow Moses, who on Mount Sinai received the Law, God's irrevocable command, obedience to which is ever the only way to salvation."

34. Similarly today, Papists, Anabaptists and other sects make outcry: "What mean you by preaching so much about faith and Christ? Are the people thereby made better? Surely works are essential." Arguments of this character have indeed a semblance of merit, but, when examined by the light of truth, are mere empty, worthless twaddle. For if deeds, or works, are to be considered, there are the Ten Commandments; we teach and practice these as well as they. The Commandments would answer the purpose indeed--if one could preach them so effectively as to compel their fulfilment. But the question is, whether what is preached is also practiced. Is there something more than were words--or letters, as Paul says? Do the words result in life and spirit? This message we have in common; unquestionably, one must teach the Ten Commandments, and, what is more, live them. But we charge that they are not observed. Therefore something else is requisite in order to render obedience to them possible. When Moses and the Law are made to say: "You should do thus; God demands this of you," what does it profit? Ay, beloved Moses, I hear that plainly, and it is certainly a righteous command; but pray tell me whence shall I obtain ability to do what, alas, I never have done nor can do? It is not easy to spend money from an empty pocket, or to drink from an empty can. If I am to pay my debt, or to quench my thirst, tell me how first to fill pocket or can. But upon this point such prattlers are silent; they but continue to drive and plague with the Law, let the people stick to their sins, and make merry of them to their own hurt.

35. In this light Paul here portrays the false apostles and like pernicious schismatics, who make great boasts of having a clearer understanding and of knowing much better what to teach than is the case with true preachers of the Gospel. And when they do their very best, when they pretend great things, and

do wonders with their preaching, there is naught but the mere empty "letter." Indeed, their message falls far short of Moses. Moses was a noble preacher, truly, and wrought greater things than any of them may do. Nevertheless, the doctrine of the Law could do no more than remain a letter, an Old Testament, and God had to ordain a different doctrine, a New Testament, which should impart the "spirit."

"It is the letter," says Paul, "which we preach. If any glorying is to be done, we can glory in better things and make the defiant plea that they are not the only teachers of what ought to be done, incapable as they are of carrying out their own precepts. We give direction and power as to performing and living those precepts. For this reason our message is not called the Old Testament, or the message of the dead letter, but that of the New Testament and of the living Spirit."

36. No seditious spirit, it is certain, ever carries out its own precepts, nor will he ever be capable of doing so, though he may loudly boast the Spirit alone as his guide. Of this fact you may rest assured. For such individuals know nothing more than the doctrine of works--nor can they rise higher and point you to anything else. They may indeed speak of Christ, but it is only to hold him up as an example of patience in suffering. In short, there can be no New Testament preached if the doctrine of faith in Christ be left out; the spirit cannot enter into the heart, but all teaching, endeavor, reflection, works and power remain mere "letters," devoid of grace, truth, and life. Without Christ the heart remains unchanged and unrenewed. It has no more power to fulfil the Law than the book in which the Ten Commandments are written, or the stones upon which engraved. "For the letter killeth, but the spirit giveth life."

37. Here is yet stronger condemnation of the glory of the doctrine of the Law; yet higher exaltation of the Gospel ministry. Is the apostle overbold in that he dares thus to assail the Law and say: "The Law is not only a lifeless letter, but qualified merely to kill"? Surely that is not calling the Law a good and profitable message, but one altogether harmful. Who, unless he would be a cursed heretic in the eyes of the world and invite execution as a blasphemer, would dare to speak thus, except Paul himself? Even Paul must praise the Law, which is God's command, declaring it good and not to be despised nor in any way modified, but to be confirmed and fulfilled so completely, as Christ says (Mt 5:18), that not a tittle of it shall pass away. How, then, does Paul come to speak so disparagingly, even abusively, of the Law, actually presenting it as veritable death and poison? Well, his is a sublime doctrine, one that reason does not understand. The world, particularly they who would be called holy and godly, cannot tolerate it at all; for it amounts to nothing short of pronouncing all our works, however precious, mere death and poison.

38. Paul's purpose is to bring about the complete overthrow of the boast of the false teachers and hypocrites, and to reveal the weakness of their doctrine, showing how little it effects even at its best, since it offers only the Law, Christ

remaining unproclaimed and unknown. They say in terms of vainglorious eloquence that if a man diligently keep the commandments and do many good works, he shall be saved. But theirs are only vain words, a pernicious doctrine. This fact is eventually learned by him who, having heard no other doctrine, trusts in their false one. He finds out that it holds neither comfort nor power of life, but only doubt and anxiety, followed by death and destruction.

Terrors of the Law

39. When man, conscious of his failure to keep God's command, is constantly urged by the Law to make payment of his debt and confronted with nothing but the terrible wrath of God and eternal condemnation, he cannot but sink into despair over his sins. Such is the inevitable consequence where the Law alone is taught with a view to attaining heaven thereby. The vanity of such trust in works is illustrated in the case of the noted hermit mentioned in Vitae Patrum. (Lives of the Fathers). For over seventy years this hermit had led a life of utmost austerity, and had many followers. When the hour of death came he began to tremble, and for three days was in a state of agony. His disciples came to comfort him, exhorting him to die in peace since he had led so holy a life. But he replied: "Alas, I truly have all my life served Christ and lived austerely; but God's judgment greatly differs from that of men."

40. Note, this worthy man, despite the holiness of his life, has no acquaintance with any article but that of the divine judgment according to the Law. He knows not the comfort of Christ's Gospel. After a long life spent in the attempt to keep God's commandments and secure salvation, the Law now slays him through his own works. He is compelled to exclaim: "Alas, who knows how God will look upon my efforts? Who may stand before him?" That means, to forfeit heaven through the verdict of his own conscience. The work he has wrought and his holiness of life avail nothing. They merely push him deeper into death, since he is without the solace of the Gospel, while others, such as the thief on the cross and the publican, grasp the comfort of the Gospel, the forgiveness of sins in Christ. Thus sin is conquered; they escape the sentence of the Law, and pass through death into life eternal.

Efficacy of the Gospel

41. Now the meaning of the contrasting clause, "the spirit giveth life," becomes clear. The reference is to naught else but the holy Gospel, a message of healing and salvation; a precious, comforting word. It comforts and refreshes the sad heart. It wrests it out of the jaws of death and hell, as it were, and transports it to the certain hope of eternal life, through faith in Christ. When the last hour comes to the believer, and death and God's judgment appear before his eyes, he does not base his comfort upon his works. Even though he may have lived the holiest life possible, he says with Paul (1 Cor. 4:4): "I know nothing against myself, yet am I not hereby justified."

42. These words imply being ill pleased with self, with the whole life, indeed, even the putting to death of self. Though the heart says, "By my works I am neither made righteous nor saved," which is practically admitting oneself to be worthy of death and condemnation, the Spirit extricates from despair, through the Gospel faith, which confesses, as did St. Bernard in the hour of death: "Dear Lord Jesus, I am aware that my life at its best has been but worthy of condemnation, but I trust in the fact that thou hast died for me and hast sprinkled me with blood from thy holy wounds. For I have been baptized in thy name and have given heed to thy Word whereby thou hast called me, awarded me grace and life, and bidden me believe. In this assurance will I pass out of life; not in uncertainty and anxiety, thinking, 'Who knows what sentence God in heaven will pass upon me?'"

The Christian must not utter such a question. The sentence against his life and works has long since been passed by the Law. Therefore, he must confess himself guilty and condemned. But he lives by the gracious judgment of God declared from heaven, whereby the sentence of the Law is overruled and reversed. It is this: "He that believeth on the Son hath eternal life" (Jn. 3:36).

43. When the consolation of the Gospel has once been received and it has wrested the heart from death and the terrors of hell, the Spirit's influence is felt. By its power God's Law begins to live in man's heart; he loves it, delights in it and enters upon its fulfilment. Thus eternal life begins here, being continued forever and perfected in the life to come.

44. Now you see how much more glorious, how much better, is the doctrine of the apostles--the New Testament--than the doctrine of those who preach merely great works and holiness without Christ. We should see in this fact an incentive to hear the Gospel with gladness. We ought joyfully to thank God for it when we learn how it has power to bring to men life and eternal salvation, and when it gives us assurance that the Holy Spirit accompanies it and is imparted to believers.

"But if the ministration of death, written, and engraven on stones, came with glory, so that the children of Israel could not look stedfastly upon the face of Moses for the glory of his face; which glory was passing away: how shall not rather the ministration of the Spirit be with glory? For if the ministration of condemnation hath glory, much rather doth the ministration of righteousness exceed in glory."

Glory of the Gospel

45. Paul is in an ecstasy of delight, and his heart overflows in words of praise for the Gospel. Again he handles the Law severely, calling it a ministration, or doctrine, of death and condemnation. What term significant of greater abomination could he apply to God's Law than to call it a doctrine of death and hell? And again (Gal 2:17), he calls it a "minister (or preacher) of sin;" and (Gal 3:10) the message which proclaims a curse, saying, "As many as are

of the works of the law are under a curse." Absolute, then, is the conclusion that Law and works are powerless to justify before God; for how can a doctrine proclaiming only sin, death and condemnation justify and save?

46. Paul is compelled to speak thus, as we said above because of the infamous presumption of both teachers and pupils, in that they permit flesh and blood to coquet with the Law, and make their own works which they bring before God their boast. Yet, nothing is effected but self-deception and destruction. For, when the Law is viewed in its true light, when its "glory," as Paul has it, is revealed, it is found to do nothing more than to kill man and sink him into condemnation.

47. Therefore, the Christian will do well to learn this text of Paul and have an armor against the boasting of false teachers, and the torments and trials of the devil when he urges the Law and induces men to seek righteousness in their own works, tormenting their heart with the thought that salvation is dependent upon the achievements of the individual. The Christian will do well to learn this text, I say, so that in such conflicts he may take the devil's own sword, saying: "Why dost thou annoy me with talk of the Law and my works? What is the Law after all, however much you may preach it to me, but that which makes me feel the weight of sin, death and condemnation? Why should I seek therein righteousness before God?"

48. When Paul speaks of the "glory of the Law," of which the Jewish teachers of work-righteousness boast, he has reference to the things narrated in the twentieth and thirtyfourth chapters of Exodus--how, when the Law was given, God descended in majesty and glory from heaven, and there were thunderings and lightnings, and the mountain was encircled with fire; and how when Moses returned from the Mountain, bringing the Law, his face shone with a glory so dazzling that the people could not look upon his face and he was obliged to veil it.

49. Turning their glory against them, Paul says: "Truly, we do not deny the glory; splendor and majesty were there: but what does such glory do but compel souls to flee before God, and drive into death and hell? We believers, however, boast another glory,--that of our ministration. The Gospel record tells us (Mt 17:2-4) that Christ clearly revealed such glory to his disciples when his face shone as the sun, and Moses and Elijah were present. Before the manifestation of such glory, the disciples did not flee; they beheld with amazed joy and said: "Lord, it is good for us to be here. We will make here tabernacles for thee and for Moses," etc.

50. Compare the two scenes and you will understand plainly the import of Paul's words here. As before said, this is the substance of his meaning: "The Law produces naught but terror and death when it dazzles the heart with its glory and stands revealed in its true nature. On the other hand, the Gospel yields comfort and joy." But to explain in detail the signification of the veiled face of Moses, and of his shining uncovered face, would take too long to enter

upon here.

51. There is also especial comfort to be derived from Paul's assertion that the "ministration," or doctrine, of the Law "passeth away"; for otherwise there would be naught but eternal condemnation. The doctrine of the Law "passes away" when the preaching of the Gospel of Christ finds place. To Christ, Moses shall yield, that he alone may hold sway. Moses shall not terrify the conscience of the believer. When, perceiving the glory of Moses, the conscience trembles and despairs before God's wrath, then it is time for Christ's glory to shine with its gracious, comforting light into the heart. Then can the heart endure Moses and Elijah. For the glory of the Law, or the unveiled face of Moses, shall shine only until man is humbled and driven to desire the blessed countenance of Christ. If you come to Christ, you shall no longer hear Moses to your fright and terror; you shall hear him as one who remains servant to the Lord Christ, leaving the solace and the joy of his countenance unobscured. In conclusion:

"For verily that which hath been made glorious hath not been made glorious in this respect, by reason of the glory that surpasseth."

52. The meaning here is; When the glory and holiness of Christ, revealed through the preaching of the Gospel, is rightly perceived then the glory of the Law--which is but a feeble and transitory glory--is seen to be not really glorious. It is mere dark clouds in contrast to the light of Christ shining to lead us out of sin, death and hell unto God and eternal life.

The Parable of the Sower

The Disciples & the Fruits of God's Word

LUKE 8:4-15: And when much people were gathered together, and were come to him out of every city, he spake by a parable: A sower went out to sow his seed: and as he sowed, some fell by the way side; and it was trodden down, and the fowls of the air devoured it. And some fell upon a rock; and as soon as it was sprung up, it withered away, because it lacked moisture. And some fell among thorns; and the thorns sprang up with it, and choked it. And other fell on good ground, and sprang up, and bare fruit an hundredfold. And when he had said these things, he cried, He that hath ears to hear, let him hear. And his disciples asked him, saying, What might this parable be? And he said, Unto you it is given to know the mysteries of the kingdom of God: but to others in parables; that seeing they might not see, and hearing they might not understand. Now the parable is this: The seed is the word of God. Those by the way side are they that hear; then cometh the devil, and taketh away the word out of their hearts, lest they should believe and be saved. They on the rock are they, which, when they hear, receive the word with joy; and these have no root, which for a while believe, and in time of temptation fall away. And that which fell among thorns are they, which, when they have heard, go forth, and are choked with cares and riches and pleasures of this life, and bring no fruit to perfection. But that on the good ground are they, which in an honest and good heart, having heard the word, keep it, and bring forth fruit with patience..

Section I. the Nature of the Word Spoken Here.

1. This Gospel treats of the disciples and the fruits, which the Word of God develops in the world. It does not speak of the law nor of human institutions; but, as Christ himself says, of the Word of God, which he himself the sower preaches, for the law bears no fruit, just as little as do the institutions of men. Christ however sets forth here four kinds of disciples of the divine Word.

Section II. The Disciples of this Word.

2. The first class of disciples are those who hear the Word but neither understand nor esteem it. And these are not the mean people in the world, but

the greatest, wisest and the most saintly, in short they are the greatest part of mankind; for Christ does not speak here of those who persecute the Word nor of those who fail to give their ear to it, but of those who hear it and are students of it, who also wish to be called true Christians and to live in Christian fellowship with Christians and are partakers of baptism and the Lord's Supper. But they are of a carnal heart, and remain so, failing to appropriate the Word of God to themselves, it goes in one ear and out the other. Just like the seed along the wayside did not fall into the earth, but remained lying on the ground in the wayside, because the road was tramped hard by the feet of man and beast and it could not take root.

3. Therefore Christ says the devil cometh and taketh away the Word from their heart, that they may not believe and be saved. What power of Satan this alone reveals, that hearts, hardened through a worldly mind and life, lose the Word and let it go, so that they never understand or confess it; but instead of the Word of God Satan sends false teachers to tread it under foot by the doctrines of men. For it stands here written both that it was trodden under foot, and the birds of the heaven devoured it. The birds Christ himself interprets as the messengers of the devil, who snatch away the Word and devour it, which is done when he turns and blinds their hearts so that they neither understand nor esteem it, as St. Paul says in 2 Tim 4:4: "They will turn away their ears from the truth, and turn aside unto fables." By the treading under foot of men Christ means the teachings of men, that rule in our hearts, as he says in Mt 5:13 also of the salt that has lost its savor, it is cast out and trodden under foot, of men; that is, as St. Paul says in 2 Ths. 2:11, they must believe a lie because they have not been obedient to the truth.

4. Thus all heretics, fanatics and sects belong to this number, who understand the Gospel in a carnal way and explain it as they please, to suit their own ideas, all of whom hear the Gospel and yet they bear no fruit, yea, more, they are governed by Satan and are harder oppressed by human institutions than they were before they heard the Word. For it is a dreadful utterance that Christ here gives that the devil taketh away the Word from their hearts, by which he clearly proves that the devil rules mightily in their hearts, notwithstanding they are called Christians and hear the Word. Likewise it sounds terribly that they are to be trodden under foot, and must be subject unto men and to their ruinous teachings, by which under the appearance and name of the Gospel the devil takes the Word from them, so that they may never believe and be saved, but must be lost forever; as the fanatical spirits of our day do in all lands. For where this Word is not, there is no salvation, and great works or holy lives avail nothing, for [it is] with this, that he says: "They shall not be saved," since they have not the Word, he shows forcibly enough, that not their works but their faith in the Word alone saves, as Paul says to the Romans: "It is, the power of God unto salvation to every one that believeth" (Rom 1:16).

5. The second class of hearers are those who receive the Word with joy, but

they do not persevere. These are also a large multitude who understand the Word correctly and lay hold of it in its purity without any spirit of sect, division or fanaticism, they rejoice also in that they know the real truth, and are able to know how they may be saved without works through faith. They also know that they are free from the bondage of the law, of their conscience and of human teachings; but when it comes to the test that they must suffer harm, disgrace and loss of life or property, then they fall and deny it; for they have not root enough, and are not planted deep enough in the soil. Hence they are like the growth on a rock, which springs forth fresh and green, that it is a pleasure to behold it and it awakens bright hopes. But when the sun shines hot it withers, because it has no soil and moisture, and only rock is there. So these do; in times of persecution they deny or keep silence about the Word, and work, speak and suffer all that their persecutors mention or wish, who formerly went forth and spoke, and confessed with a fresh and joyful spirit the same, while there was still peace and no heat, so that there was hope they would bear much fruit and serve the people. For these fruits are not only the works, but more the confession, preaching and spreading of the Word, so that many others may thereby be converted and the kingdom of God be developed.

6. The third class are those who hear and understand the Word, but still it falls on the other side of the road, among the pleasures and cares of this life, so that they also do nothing with the Word. And there is quite a large multitude of these; for although they do not start heresies, like the first, but always possess the absolutely pure Word, they are also, not attacked on the left as the others with opposition and persecution; yet they fall on the right side, and it is their ruin that they enjoy peace and good days. Therefore they do not earnestly give themselves to the Word, but become indifferent and sink in the cares, riches and pleasures of this life, so that they are of no benefit to any one. Therefore they are like the seed that fell among the thorns. Although it is not rocky but good soil; not wayside but deeply plowed soil; yet, the thorns will not let it spring up, they choke it. Thus these have all in the Word that is needed for their salvation, but they do not make any use of it, and they rot in this life in carnal pleasures. To these belong those who hear the Word but do not bring under subjection their flesh. They know their duty but do it not, they teach but do not practice what they teach, and are this year as they were last.

7. The fourth class are those who lay hold of and keep the Word in a good and honest heart, and bring forth fruit with patience, those who hear the Word and steadfastly retain it, meditate upon it and act in harmony with it. The devil does not snatch it away, nor are they thereby led astray, moreover the heat of persecution does not rob them of it, and the thorns of pleasure and the avarice of the times do not hinder its growth; but they bear fruit by teaching others and by developing the kingdom of God, hence they also do good to their neighbor in love; and therefore Christ adds, "they bring forth fruit with patience." For these must suffer much on account of the Word, shame and disgrace from fanatics

and heretics, hatred and jealousy with injury to body and property from their persecutors, not to mention what the thorns and the temptations of their own flesh do, so that it may well be called the Word of the cross; for he who would keep it must bear the cross and misfortune, and triumph. field,

8. He says: "In honest and good hearts." Like a field that is without a thorn or brush, cleared and spacious, as a beautiful clean place: so a heart is also cleared and clean, broad and spacious, that is without cares and avarice as to temporal needs, so that the Word of God truly finds lodgment there. But the field is good, not only when it lies there cleared and level, but when it is also rich and fruitful, possesses soil and is productive, and not like a stony and gravelly field. Just so is the heart that has good soil and with a full spirit is strong, fertile and good to keep the Word and bring forth fruit with patience.

9. Here we see why it is no wonder there are so few true Christians, for all the seed does not fall into good ground, but only the fourth and small part; and that they are not to be trusted who boast they are Christians and praise the teaching of the Gospel; like Demas, a disciple of St. Paul, who forsook him at last (2 Tim. 4:10); like the disciples of Jesus, who turned their backs to him (John 6:66). For Christ himself cries out here: "He that hath ears to hear, let him hear," as if he should say: O, how few true Christians there are; one dare not believe all to be Christians who are called Christians and hear the Gospel, more is required than that.

10. All this is spoken for our instruction, that we may not go astray, since so many misuse the Gospel and few lay hold of it aright. True it is unpleasant to preach to those who treat the Gospel so shamefully and even oppose it. For preaching is to become so universal that the Gospel is to be proclaimed to all creatures, as Christ says in Mk. 16:15: "Preach the Gospel to the whole creation;" and Ps. 19:4: "Their line is gone out through all the earth, and their words to the end of the world." What business is it of mine that many do not esteem it? It must be that many are called but few are chosen. For the sake of the good ground that brings forth fruit with patience, the seed must also fall fruitless by the wayside, on the rock and among the thorns; inasmuch as we are assured that the Word of God does not go forth without bearing some fruit, but it always finds also good ground; as Christ says here, some seed of the sower falls also into good ground, and not only by the wayside, among the thorns and on stony ground. For wherever the Gospel goes you will find Christians. "My word shall not return unto me void" (Is. 55:11).

Section IV. Why Christ Calls the Doctrine Concerning the Disciples and the Fruits of the Word a Mystery.

19. But what does it mean when he says: "Unto you it is given to know the mysteries of the kingdom of God", etc.? What are the mysteries? Shall one not

know them, why then are they preached? A "mystery" is a hidden secret, that is not known: and the "mysteries of the kingdom of God" are the things in the kingdom of God, as for example Christ with all his grace, which he manifests to us, as Paul describes him; for he who knows Christ aright understands what God's kingdom is, and what is in it. And it is called a mystery because it is spiritual and secret, and indeed it remains so, where the spirit does not reveal it. For although there are many who see and hear it, yet they do not understand it. just as there are many who preach and hear Christ, how he offered himself for us; but all that is only upon their tongue and not in their heart; for they themselves do not believe it, they do not experience it, as Paul in 1 Cor. 2:14 says: "The natural man receiveth not the things of the Spirit of God!" Therefore Christ says here: "Unto you it is given", the Spirit gives it to you that you not only hear and see it, but acknowledge and believe it with your heart. Therefore it is now no longer a mystery to you. But to the others who hear it as well as you, and have no faith in their heart, they see and understand it not; to them it is a mystery and it will continue unknown to them, and all that they hear is only like one hearing a parable or a dark saying. This is also proved by the fanatics of our day, who know so much to preach about Christ; but as they themselves do not experience it in their heart, they rush ahead and pass by the true foundation of the mystery and tramp around with questions and rare foundlings, and when it comes to the test they do not know the least thing about trusting in God and finding in Christ the forgiveness of their sins.

20. But Mark says (4:33), Christ spake therefore to the people with parables, that they might understand, each according to his ability. How does that agree with what Matthew says, 13:13-14: He spake therefore unto them in parables, because they did not understand? It must surely be that Mark wishes to say that parables serve to the end that they may get a hold of coarse, rough people, although they do not indeed understand them, yet later, they may be taught and then they know: for parables are naturally pleasing to the common people, and they easily remember them since they are taken from common every day affairs, in the midst of which the people live. But Matthew means to say that these parables are of the nature that no one can understand them, they may grasp and hear them as often as they will, unless the Spirit makes them known and reveals them. Not that they should preach that we shall not understand them; but it naturally follows that wherever the Spirit does not reveal them, no one understands them. However, Christ took these words from Is. 6:9-10, where the high meaning of the divine foreknowledge is referred to, that God conceals and reveals to whom he will and whom he had in mind from eternity.

Made in the USA
Columbia, SC
11 December 2017